AROUND THE WORLD WITH

ONE DIRECTION

THE TRUE STORIES AS TOLD BY THE FANS

SARAH OLIVER

JOHN BLAKE

Published by John Blake Publishing Ltd,
3 Bramber Court, 2 Bramber Road,
London W14 9PB, England

www.johnblakepublishing.co.uk

www.facebook.com/Johnblakepub facebook
twitter.com/johnblakepub twitter

First published in paperback in 2013

ISBN: 978 1 78219 444 6

British Library Cataloguing-in-Publication Data:

A catalogue record for this book is available from the British Library.

Design by www.envydesign.co.uk

Printed and bound in Great Britain by CPI Group (UK) Ltd

1 3 5 7 9 10 8 6 4 2

© Text copyright Sarah Oliver 2013

Papers used by John Blake Publishing are natural, recyclable products made
from wood grown in sustainable forests. The manufacturing processes
conform to the environmental regulations of the country of origin.

Every attempt has been made to contact the relevant copyright-holders,
but some were unobtainable. We would be grateful if the appropriate people
could contact us.

Dedicated to Courtney

CONTENTS

INTRODUCTION

S arah Oliver is an author from Widnes in Cheshire. She was the author of the first ever book on Harry, Niall, Liam, Louis and Zayn, entitled *One Direction A-Z*, which was a *Sunday Times* bestseller. She also wrote the double biography of Harry Styles and Niall Horan, and appeared in the documentary *One Direction All For One*.

Why not follow Sarah – @SarahOliverAtoZ – on Twitter?

As you read this book, you will hear stories of when fans met Harry, Niall, Liam, Louis and Zayn (and when they met their bodyguards too!). You'll find out what the boys think of the different countries they visit and the flash mobs that fans do for them. The boys have spent lots of time in America, but they have been to lots of other countries too – after all, they are the world's biggest boyband! They want to visit every single country so they can thank Directioners everywhere for their support. It might take them a few years but they'll do it one day.

The boys' tour manager and head of security is Paul Higgins from Ireland and all the boys are very close to him. Paul used to work with former *X Factor* winner Shayne Ward, Girls Aloud, Boyzone and Westlife. He keeps the boys safe in the different countries they visit. One of their bodyguards (until late 2012) was Andy Davies and many fans were gutted when he changed jobs. He had looked after the boys for nine months as they travelled around the world. The boys used to call him 'Baldy' and he would stand guard outside their hotel rooms to make sure that no fans disturbed the boys through the night.

You'll also find out what the boys' families are like from fans who've met them at concerts, signings and the hotels that the boys stay in while they're away from home. Some fans queue up for days to get wristbands so they can attend signings; others send their dads to stand in line for them. You'll read all about the challenges fans had to do to win Go1Den Tickets to meet the boys in New York, and you'll also find out what happens when fans wait for the boys outside recording studios. Harry, Niall, Liam, Louis and Zayn love all their fans, but there are some fans that are more like friends to the boys, as they have met them so many times and they know they can have a laugh with them. The boys love messing around and play fighting, and are so grateful when they receive artwork and unique gifts from the different countries they visit.

So what are you waiting for? Let's go around the world and follow in One Direction's footsteps!

CHAPTER ONE

AMERICA

As soon as *The X Factor* was over and the band had finished in third place, they were whisked off to LA by their record label. This was a huge deal because they were going to be recording with some of the best people in the record business. The boys had never expected things to go so fast – it's a good job they all had passports, so could jump on a plane!

Sonny Takhar, the chief executive officer of Syco Records, explained to *Music Week*, 'We started working with the band immediately after the show had finished – they went to LA and recorded with RedOne. Then, while the boys were out on *The X Factor* tour between February and April, we started finding and sourcing songs and creating situations where songs were written for the boys in preparation for them to record once they had finished.'

The boys love America. When Marie Morreale interviewed them for the Scholastic blog, she asked them what their first impressions of America were.

'I really like it because it's really hot over there and the people are actually really nice,' Liam replied. 'So when you go to a restaurant and stuff and you...'

'Even people in the street,' Harry interrupted.

'Yeah, people in the street as well,' Liam continued, 'but in the restaurants, they're always asking like...'

'Hey, how you doing?' Harry finished his sentence.

'The common line in Florida after you finish your meal is, "Have a good day," which is amazing, I think,' said Liam. 'You don't really hear that in the UK.'

The boys never thought that they would break America; they just thought they would be big in the UK and Ireland, so when they found out that their record company wanted to take them to the States, they were blown away. Even established UK artists with lots of number-one singles under their belts have flopped in America, but this wasn't going to happen to our favourite five lads. 'We're just five normal boys from the UK who've been given this opportunity,' Harry confessed to *The AP*, 'so we're having a great time working very hard.'

Before the boys went over to America, their record

company used social media to build a fan base and to get people talking about them. 'Twitter, Facebook and YouTube have been a large percentage of the reason we've been known outside of the UK. We owe a massive thank you to the fans,' Harry explained.

A website was set up called (www.bring1dtous.com) and fans had to compete to win a visit by One Direction to their city. The website stated, 'Are you ready to bring 1D to your city? Visit www.Bring1DtoUS.com now to get started on the first challenge. Click on your city for directions about how you can earn points for your city. Each challenge will bring you one step closer to a special 1D event in your city!'

The winning city was Dallas in Texas and the boys arrived on 24 March 2012. Demand for wristbands for the event was so high that the venue had to change from Stonebriar Centre Mall to the much bigger Dr Pepper Ballpark, home of the Frisco RoughRiders baseball team. Fans could get a signed copy of *Up All Night* and watch One Direction perform.

On 21 March 2012, American Directioners found out the *Up All Night Tour* was going to be expanded to include 26 North American dates in May and June. The fans were thrilled and rushed out to get tickets as soon as they could. The band's friend Olly Murs, who had been runner-up in the 2009 series of *The X*

Factor, and Filipino-American singer Manika supported the boys.

DID YOU KNOW?

While she was on tour with them, Manika admitted in an interview that the boys had taught her some British slang words and that Zayn liked to drive a mini-scooter from the boys' dressing room to the canteen and back.

When the boys were embarking on their first tour of America, they invited Radio 1 to go with them. Harry, Niall, Louis, Liam and Zayn were supporting American band Big Time Rush at ten gigs in February 2012 before going on their own tour. Before their Nashville gig, the boys were staying at the Sheraton Hotel, Tennessee. 'I'm sat in a hotel room at the moment, having my hair done because I have a lot of hair,' Harry told the Radio 1 crew. 'We're doing today a Nickelodeon bit of promo, so a little bit of makeup never hurt anyone. Tonight we're playing in Nashville. I think we're meeting some country singers. We're meeting Martina McBride and Faith Hill, who are coming to the show. They're gonna bring their kids to a, like, meet and greet, so that should be fun.'

On a typical day on tour, the boys wake up

somewhere new, catch up on a couple of hours' sleep in a hotel room, have a shower, grab some breakfast and then jump on the tour bus. Then they get their hair/makeup done and head to a radio or television station for some interviews before going to the arena in which they will be performing that night. They might have a sound check, meet some fans, then have something to eat before heading on stage. After their performance, it is usually late and they have to jump back on the tour bus and be driven to a new city and a new hotel. They are literally on the go from the minute they get up in the morning until very late at night. They don't usually arrive at their new hotel until the early hours of the morning, but they still take time out to chat to any fans that are waiting there to see them. Some days they work for 20 or more hours!

DID YOU KNOW?

If Niall had to choose between sleeping in a posh hotel room or sleeping on the 1D tour bus, he would pick the tour bus every time. He doesn't mind sleeping in his bus bunk and he can play computer games or Skype his brother Greg or friends at home in Ireland. When the boys stay in a hotel, they are only there for a couple of nights max because so many fans turn up to try and catch a glimpse of them. Sometimes when they arrive, their security team have to call the police to control the crowds and allow One Direction to get inside.

The tour bus the boys had for the Big Time Rush tour was really big but the boys didn't keep it very clean. Many times the driver would have to pull over at fast-food restaurants because they were feeling peckish. They would order something and then take it back on the bus to eat. Sometimes they ended up having wrestling matches halfway through eating, so fries would end up everywhere. Niall thinks Louis is the messiest and is usually to blame for starting the wrestling matches.

For the boys it was really special when they performed some of their first gigs in the States and heard the girls in the audience singing their words back to them. They didn't expect it at all, and they loved seeing banners that fans had made. It was clear that some of the banners had taken hours to make as they were very detailed and included sketches of each boy's face, as well as the twitter names of the fans who had made them.

DID YOU KNOW?

When the boys are touring they have to eat a lot more than they usually would because their shows are physically demanding (even though they don't do big dance routines like some bands). They need to make sure they have loads of energy.

After the boys performed in Nashville, they had to tidy their tour bus and then catch a flight to New York at 5 a.m. They went to the *Big Time Movie* premiere and then the next day to Z100, the biggest radio station in New York, for an interview, to perform and to meet some fans. When they performed on *The Today Show* a few days later, they had to be up at 5 a.m. again. It was their first interview on USA TV. The boys arrived on a big red bus and so many fans turned up to see them. During their interview they said the thing they liked most about American girls is that they are loud.

DID YOU KNOW?

Harry, Niall, Liam, Louis and Zayn performed on *The Today Show* again, in November 2012, and even more fans turned up. In fact, the presenter

Matt Lauer said, 'We have never, ever had a crowd this big. This one breaks all the records.' More than 15,000 saw them perform their new single 'Little Things', as well as 'What Makes You Beautiful' and 'Live While We're Young'. Niall told them, 'We are going to do our first ever movie and it's going to be in 3D and it's coming to cinemas near you on 30 August 2013.' This made the fans scream even louder!

1D superfan Nikki was at the boys' *Today Show* appearance and managed to meet Niall's family. 'We ended up very close to the stage and right next to the barrier across from where the boys exited and entered,' she said. 'After the sound check, we were all talking and a man in VIP asked my friend Erin who her favourite was. She showed him her sign: NIALL, I'M 100 PER CENT IRISH, and said, "Niall, of course!" He laughed and replied, "Oh, my nephew." Then he pointed to the women beside him and said, "This is his mum."

'We were all a little shocked with everything, you could say. I looked at the woman and realised she'd taken a picture of my sign earlier. She took a few more pictures of our friends and our signs and then we talked to them. My friend Erin began talking to them about Ireland. I made a complete fool out of myself, dropping my sign a few times and asking Maura – Niall's mom – if she knew Zayn's mom. Out of all the questions I could have asked her, I asked if she knew Zayn's mom. I guess it was because I wasn't thinking clearly. But the whole time Niall's family were very nice. You could tell they were very proud of Niall. Then the boys came out and performed and after that we said our goodbyes and left.'

DID YOU KNOW?

Niall had a bad experience with a pigeon when he was younger: it flew through a window when he was on the toilet and he has been scared of them ever since. The *Sun* newspaper reported that the boys had extra security while they were touring the US to stop any pigeons from getting close to Niall.

Whenever the boys are in New York, Niall tries to catch up with his cousins who live there. One of his cousins is called Annie and he has two more, each called Katie. His cousins went to the boys' first signing in the city, along with more than 1,000 fans. Their first album, *Up All Night*, was actually released in America while the boys were in New York. The album came out a week earlier than had been planned because they were so popular, with fans rushing out to buy it on 13 March 2012. Some fans at the signing bought multiple copies. On the day of its release, the deluxe version was number one and the standard version reached number two. The night before it came out, Niall received a well-done tweet from Katy Perry. He explained to Radio 1, 'When I auditioned for *The X Factor*, Katy Perry was the guest judge and she was the last judge to put me through, and when she put me through, she said, "OK, don't let me down," and I said, "I won't," and then she tweeted me last night: "Congratulations you didn't let me down." I went crazy... not very often do you get a tweet from Katy Perry, so I was a bit excited.'

The album did even better in America than it did in the UK, taking the number-one spot on the Billboard 200 chart. The boys sold an incredible 176,000 copies in the first week alone, making them the first UK/Ireland group to achieve this with their debut album.

DID YOU KNOW?

During the boys' tour of America with Big Time Rush, they had B12 vitamin injections in their bottoms to help their immune systems and to give them energy. They were so in demand that they couldn't afford to be ill and take days off. Harry told BBC Radio 1, 'In the UK your biggest travel [between gigs] is 4 hours and here it's 14 hours. It's a bit strange, struggling to adapt but you know we'll be all good.'

Niall found out that the album was number one in America when he was travelling in a cab. He admitted to CKO196.9 Radio, 'I was in the back of a cab and I was going to Sony music to collect my tickets. I was going to a basketball game and I was with my friend, and my manager called me up and told me we were number one. And I went crazy, I screamed my head off and the taxi driver nearly kicked me out of the car. He was freaked out.'

Harry told MTV, 'We simply cannot believe that we are number one in America! It's beyond a dream come true for us. We want to thank each and every one of our fans in the US who bought our album and we would also like to thank the American public for being so supportive of us.'

Niall added, 'We just found out that we are number one in America and as you can imagine, we are over the moon!'

The boys' first single release from *Up All Night* was

'What Makes You Beautiful' and it was released in America on Valentine's Day 2012. It was number four on the Billboard Hot 100 chart. It had been released in the UK and in Europe months earlier, on 11 September 2011. The video for 'What Makes You Beautiful' was the boys' first proper music video as a band. It was filmed on a beach in Malibu, California. Liam's dad Geoff told the *Express & Star*, 'The lads went over to California in July. They were over there for two weeks while they shot the video. They spent three days on the beach shooting the scenes. It was tough work.

'The days were 18 hours long. The first three days over there, they spent getting to know the girls in their video. They went to a funfair so that when they came to shoot, they would feel comfortable with each other.'

In the 'What Makes You Beautiful' video, the boys ride around in an orange camper van driven by Louis. The story of the video is that the boys are meeting up with three girls. They go to the beach and it is revealed that Harry has fallen for one of the girls, who doesn't know she is beautiful. They have lots of fun on the beach and then when it gets dark, sit around a campfire. The actress chosen to play Harry's love interest was called Madison and Louis teased Harry by saying that Harry had fallen for her.

AMERICA

The director of the video, John Urbano, loved working with Harry, Niall, Liam, Louis and Zayn and told the backstage cameras during filming, 'The video's been going great, it's been a ton of fun. Working with the guys ... they're amazing. They work so well with each other, you know, it's like they've been best friends for ever and that's exactly what we're looking for.'

DID YOU KNOW?

Louis ended up being pulled over by cops twice because he was driving the camper van too slowly.

Wherever the boys are in the world, they get at least one day off a week so they don't burn out. Some of their craziest days off have happened while they were in America. When they had a day off in New York Liam ended up being hit in the face and his shirt was ripped. 'They couldn't see where they were going and it was really, really dangerous,' a source told the *Mirror*. 'Nearby police had to calm the girls down. They are going to have to be more careful in the future and have at least a security guard each with them. It's a shame for the boys because they appreciate their freedom.'

Liam and Niall were shaken by what happened and tweeted about being mobbed. Niall tweeted, 'This is a complete joke ... ridic ... Day off, wana chill'. And Liam tweeted, 'That wasn't even funny.'

But Niall knew that only a few fans had ruined their day off. Back in the safety of their hotel, he tweeted to let the fans outside know that he could hear them singing.

On their days off the boys like to go the cinema if they can, or to local attractions like theme parks. When they were in California, they went fishing together and Liam managed to catch a baby tiger shark. Once everyone had seen it, and those who wanted to had given it a stroke, he released it back into the ocean.

DID YOU KNOW?

Niall nearly missed a flight to America once because he was too busy eating Japanese food in an airport's Wagamama restaurant with Liam. He is a huge fan and gets excited when 1D visit a city and he finds out they have a Wagamama.

The boys' filmed their second music video in New York at the Plattsburgh campus of the State University of New York and at Lake Placid. 'Gotta Be You' was released in November 2011 in the UK, Ireland and Australia only. The video was filmed just a month before its release and shows the boys as students, leaving school and travelling to a lake to have a bonfire with some girls. Louis drives a Mini Cooper, Zayn goes by train, Liam drives a Beetle car and Harry travels there on a red scooter. Niall loved being able to play the guitar in this video. It finishes with a big fireworks display and a silhouette of Zayn walking towards his love interest and going to kiss her. To see a behind-the-scenes video, go to YouTube and type in 'Gotta Be You Video Out Takes'. You'll see the boys singing a funny song and Zayn serenading a big teddy bear.

The boys spent a lot of 2012 in America and Harry was even there for his 18th birthday on 1 February. His mum was gutted that she couldn't be there with him and tweeted, 'Happy Birthday darling! @Harry_Styles have a great day. you're very loved !!'

She also tweeted a photo, which showed some of the presents she had received from fans to pass on to Harry when he was next home. The birthday gifts included Haribo sweets, Maltesers, a canvas, a mug with 'I Love Girls' written on it, a woolly hat, T-shirts, a teddy bear and loads of cards.

Harry told his followers, 'I feel like I've woken up with suddenly more facial hair and a deeper voice ...

Thank you for all your lovely Birthday messages :D .xx'

DID YOU KNOW?

Harry was pranked on his birthday. The other boys booked him a massage at the W Hotel in Los Angeles but halfway through they ran in with four buckets of cold water and threw the water all over him.

One Direction have had many highlights during their time in America. Here are some of their favourites:

Acting in *iCarly*. The boys loved having the opportunity to act in the hit Nickelodeon show *iCarly* alongside Miranda Cosgrove. When they arrived at the studio to film their episode, they were greeted by more than 500 fans. When it was shown on TV on 7 April, 'iGo One Direction' was watched by 3.9 million people.

Afterwards a rumour started circulating that the boys were going to be given their own series but Niall soon put the record straight, telling CKO196.9 Radio, 'Since we said we were coming to America, Nickelodeon have been right with us from the start, y'know. They helped us out, y'know – we hosted their Saturday night TV shows for the whole month of

March, we did an episode of *iCarly*, they're giving us the biggest performance, the Kids Choice Awards, next week and us and Katy Perry are the only people performing, so it's very much a big deal. Nickelodeon has been really good to us but there's no TV show.'

The Baby Prank. When the boys were being interviewed by Nickelodeon, Louis and Zayn joined in a prank to make Harry, Liam and Niall think that the woman interviewing them was about to give birth. Harry completely fell for it and Louis even tried to ring his mum, who is a nurse. Harry admitted to the cameras, 'I was thinking, this is going to be a great press story – "One Direction delivers child!"'

To see the video, search on YouTube for 'One Direction Prank on Nickelodeon'.

The Up All Night Tour. It is impossible for the boys to agree on one favourite performance from the Up All Night Tour, but the last one at Fort Lauderdale, Florida was pretty special. Harry tweeted, 'Last show of the tour tonight. Thanks to an amazing crew, and everyone involved for making it what it was. Tonight will be fun.' It was the end of an era as they had finished a run of over 60 shows worldwide.

Niall tweeted after the concert, 'Wow ft,lauderdale! Great way to finish our 1st headline US tour! #upallnight tour is done! Long six months but amazing! Thank you all so much.'

MTV Video Music Awards. The boys picked up three awards at the 2012 MTV Video Music Awards in Los Angeles and Niall even got a kiss from Katy Perry. Niall and Zayn were so thrilled to win that they stayed in America for a few more days rather than fly back home with the others.

Niall told Australian radio hosts Kyle and Jackie O, 'Katy Perry had lovely purple lipstick on and I still haven't washed it off, to be fair!'

He also sent a tweet to Katy with a picture of their kiss and the message, '@katyperry looks like its official ... me and you pic.twitter.com/iYvge5Sb.' Fans of both stars loved it and it was tweeted over 77,000 times. Katy replied, 'I'll be your Mrs Robinson.' (Mrs Robinson is a character from the 1967 movie *The Graduate*, which saw a young graduate being seduced by an older woman.)

Saturday Night Live. Harry, Niall, Liam, Louis and Zayn were musical guests on the American hit comedy sketch show *Saturday Night Live* in April 2012, alongside *Modern Family* star Sofia Vergara, who was hosting the episode. More than 37 million people watch the show every week – so it was a lot bigger than the *iCarly* show.

The boys performed 'What Makes You Beautiful' and 'One Thing'. They had to wear moustaches and wigs for *The Manuel Ortiz Show* sketch, which they found really fun to do. After the show Niall tweeted, 'SNL tonight was amazing. Thanks to @nbcsnl for having us. Much appreciated!'

Harry also tweeted, saying, 'Thank you so much to @nbcsnl for having us. That was a lot of fun and we'll never forget it.'

Radio City Hall performance in New York. On 3 September 2012, the boys performed at New York's prestigious Radio City Hall. Louis told MTV, 'It was absolutely incredible to play Radio City Hall. That place has got a lot of history and it was just such an honour to play in front of that crowd.'

At the time, the Radio City Hall performance was the loudest show they had ever done. When they went to leave after the performance, fans surrounded their van, banging on the windows and jumping on the van's back bumper. It was so crazy that their security team had to force the fans back so the boys could leave without anyone getting hurt. Afterwards the boys went to a bowling alley, but they managed to break the lane machinery when they threw three bowling balls down a single lane.

Madison Square Garden. Three months later Harry, Niall, Liam, Louis and Zayn performed a headline gig at Madison Square Garden in New York. Before the night itself, Niall told the media, 'We are so happy to be playing Madison Square Garden. To be headlining our OWN show in a venue that has played host to countless legendary acts that we have grown up listening to and adore is obviously a dream come true for us all. We can't wait to play for our fans on 3 December.'

DID YOU KNOW?

One of the downsides to One Direction being a worldwide success is the awful jetlag they get when they travel from continent to continent. Niall really hates being jetlagged and tweeted on 2 September 2012, 'I dont like jet lag! He's evil ! He just threw a bucket of water over me to wake me up at 6 am!oh no that was a glass of water I spilt #wee'.

In many interviews, the boys are asked what makes American girls different from British girls. Liam thinks that American girls are very confident and Harry likes to say that British girls wear more coats. They are also often asked about their individual style. In an interview the boys did with *Teen Vogue*, Zayn described Liam's style as 'American Casual'. He described his own style as 'more urban, more street. Nike trainers, varsity jacket. Louis is a bit more "fashion". More staples: stripes, braces, really tight trousers. Harry is quite preppy.' Louis added, 'Niall is quite casual, do you think?'

When the boys were ready to start working on their second album, *Take Me Home*, they went to Los Angeles to work with record producers there. Rather than be chauffeured around every day, Harry decided to rent a luxury car – a black Ferrari California convertible. He had only passed his driving test six months earlier. To hire the car for a single day is roughly £1,400, so Harry spent quite a lot of money on renting the car during his stay.

Harry loves luxury cars and owns a Range Rover Sport and an Audi R8 Coupe. His car insurance is really high because of his age; when he bought his Range Rover Sport, it was reported that his insurance alone was £15,000. In the week leading up to his 19th birthday, he was spotted with a classic white Ford Capri.

JENNIFER'S STORY

Jennifer is 18 and from New York. She has met One Direction lots of times, along with her best friend Gemma. The first time they met the band was Friday, 9 March 2012. They queued for hours outside the radio station Z100 and were photographed by the paparazzi carrying a yellow homemade poster bearing the words ONE THING, ONE DREAM, 100 PER CENT DIRECTIONER. (A photo of them by One Direction's van actually appeared in the *Mirror* newspaper in the UK.) It was really cold but they wrapped up warm.

The girls missed seeing the boys go into the radio station because there were so many fans there but they did see them when they were leaving. 'Although we just saw them through a car window, it was totally worth it,' Jennifer says. 'I saw One Direction. Finally, after all this time, after supporting them for a year and a half. Harry was the one I saw the most and I was against Zayn's window while he was making funny faces at me. Niall even pointed at our poster and laughed. He gave it the thumbs up.

'I'm not going to lie, I did chase down the car for a little while, but eventually we stopped because we had a concert to attend. That day One Direction was opening up for Big Time Rush at Radio City Music Hall. I'd never seen them perform live before, so I basically cried for the whole time they sang. After the concert, we went straight to where they were coming out. Being as short as I am, I couldn't see anything, but I chased the car again. I had to at least see them one more time because I didn't know the next time I'd see them again.'

It turned out that Jennifer and Gemma wouldn't have long to wait at all: the boys were doing a CD signing three days later. The first 1,000 people to line up would get to meet them, so the girls camped out from 6pm the night before. They were first in line so they were really excited, waiting with the friends they had made outside Z100. They stayed up all night writing letters to Harry, Louis, Zayn, Liam and Niall.

'It's not like I would have slept anyway,' Jennifer says. 'I was too excited and the cold was unbearable. We got up at seven to walk in and get our wristbands. The anticipation was killer. When I finally bought my CD and got my wristband, I said, "I think I'm going to cry." It wasn't real. This couldn't be happening. They finally came around 2pm; we all screamed and cried. We were close to the beginning of the line, so Niall was the first one we met. We weren't allowed to bring in cameras or anything, but it was still amazing.

'No one understands how much these boys have affected my life, and meeting them, even if it was for a second, was incredible. I promised myself I wouldn't cry in front of them, but considering that Niall was first (since he is my favourite), I thought I was going to lose it. I just stood there star struck in front of Niall not knowing what to say. No matter how many things I had planned in my head, nothing would come out of my mouth. Security had to ask me if my card was for him. I finally said that it was and said hi to him and asked how he was. He said, "Hi" back, and that he

23

was good. Then he looked me in the eyes and he smiled. And then I died and told him I loved him about a million times. Then I asked for a high-five (because, unfortunately, hugs weren't allowed) and he gave me one. Security kept pushing us along.

'Next up was Zayn, then Liam. I said hello to both, they said it back, and then I got high-fives. Then I got to Louis. He said hello, but the conversation ended there because he turned to Harry and said, "Well, I guess we made it big in America." Harry smiled at him. Although I wish I got to say more to Louis, I was glad that I was the only one who witnessed that moment. They seemed really happy and proud of how far they had come. Next up was Harry. I must have said hi about 20 times, and he gave me a high-five and smiled. His eyes were so much prettier than I could have even imagined and his hands were huge. I just told him how proud I was of them and that I would always support them. He was so appreciative.'

Jennifer and Gemma also met the boys on 25 May before the performance at the Izod Center in New Jersey and the next day they saw Louis and his girlfriend Eleanor as well as the other boys. They were in the front row at their 3 December show at Madison Square Garden. All in all, they met the boys five times in 2012 – quite an achievement!

TIFFANI'S STORY

Tiffani is a One Direction fan from Boston. Tiffani and her friends Lexi, Jaki and Jordan were the first East Coast USA fans the boys ever met, and they have met ten times so far!

The first time they met, the boys had been filming their 'Gotta Be You' video on 27 September 2011. The band hadn't launched themselves in America yet but Tiffani had seen their *X Factor* performances on the Internet thanks to her friend Jaki and had been following them on Twitter. The boys had posted a picture on Facebook of them eating at a restaurant and Jaki recognised it as a place they had been to before in upstate New York. She checked and it was, so together they decided to go to New York. Tiffani drove for six hours to get them to Lake Placid, a village in Essex County, New York, but on the way to a petrol station ended up crashing the car into a ditch. Thankfully, after a half-hour wait they were back on the road again. Tiffani takes up the story...

'We were just pulling into the hotel when a van pulled in and one of my friends in the car was like, "Uhmm. I think that's them," so I made Jaki, Jordan and Lexi jump out while I parked. Turns out it was them just getting back from the video shoot. We were able to catch Harry and Liam and took a group photo. We chatted for a bit before Harry said, "Well, it was lovely to meet you but we're knackered and want to go to bed." So we said goodnight. Paul [their tour manager] came over to talk to us and told us to come back in the morning and he'd make sure we got proper time with the boys and to please not say anything about their whereabouts. So we went back the next morning.'

The boys had to leave the hotel really early the next day, so Tiffani and her friends had to be back for 5.45 a.m. – ouch. The boys were supposed to be leaving at 6.15 a.m. but they were running late. Harry and Liam were the first to come outside, followed by Niall and Zayn. Niall and Zayn were really tired; they're not morning people, as Tiffani can confirm.

'My friends called Niall over and he came over rubbing his eyes,' she recalls. 'Zayn kept walking, my friends had to call him three times before he realised he was being called. We took photos with the two of them. I asked Niall if he was tired and he said yes. The two of them are really not morning people and barely talked. So now we were just waiting to see Louis. Well, we overheard Paul talking about how late Louis was and that they'd just have to come back for him since he wasn't in the first few shots. As the van with the other four boys left, Louis finally strolled out and we called out to him and asked for a photo. He said,

"Yeah, sure!" but Paul made him get into the other car that was waiting because he was that late. So we were disappointed we didn't get to speak to Louis.

'As the car was driving away, Louis rolled down the window and yelled, "I'm really sorry, girls! I'm really late! I'm really sorry!" So we couldn't be upset for that. We went to get breakfast and in the parking lot – my car had completely died! We were supposed to be heading home. I had to call for help, wait for my car to be fixed, so we booked another night at our hotel. We went back to the hotel, started talking about our experiences online. Somehow, our car accident when we crashed into the ditch got misconstrued and the story became that *they* were in a car accident and Harry died! So yes, my friends and I *accidently* started the rumour that the boys died on their way to the second video shoot!'

That night the girls went back to the hotel because they really wanted to see Louis properly. The boys arrived back at 8.30pm; they'd had such a long day's filming. They still had time to speak to Tiffani and her friends, and the girls could take lots of photos. Zayn liked Lexi's tattoos and he talked to her about his tattoos, and then Liam started talking but he was talking in the third person. The girls asked him why and he replied, 'When Liam's tired, Liam starts talking about himself in the third person.'

27

The next time Tiffani and her friends met the boys, it was totally unexpected. It was Tuesday, 28 February 2012: the boys were on the Big Time Rush tour. Tiffani and her friends had tickets to three of the shows and the first one was in Albany, New York. The girls had booked into the Hilton, not knowing that the boys would be there. 'We didn't know until the next morning,' Tiffani reveals. 'Apparently, they showed up in the middle of the night. So when we got up and headed to the lobby, they were just checking in. We said hi to Harry as he walked in – poor thing was so tired he almost got in the "down" elevator instead of the "up" one. We also said a quick hello to Liam and Louis before they went to their rooms. Since breakfast wasn't for a while, my friends and I decided to go relax in the hot tub. While we were there, Liam had gone to the gym and some girls were creepily watching him work out so he left. Later, Paul came down and Jaki and Jordan went over to say hi while Lexi and I stayed in the hot tub. He said hello and told them, "I know you! How do I know you?" And they responded that we had met them in Lake Placid and he said, "Right! And I said I wouldn't forget you, and I didn't!"

'Later, when Lexi and I were leaving the hot tub area, we couldn't find Jaki and Jordan so we went upstairs (dripping wet, wrapped in towels) but still couldn't find them. So we had to go back to our room. Lexi literally almost head-butted Liam as he was coming off the elevator and we were getting on. Throughout the morning, we kept seeing Liam on the elevator. He kept saying that'd he'd see us again later. Meanwhile, the group of girls forming in the lobby, having figured out One Direction were there, thought we were actually *with* the boys due to Liam having told my friends he'd see them later!

'When we came down for breakfast, Liam and Niall were seated right across from us. We decided to just leave them alone and let them eat and not say anything to them. We know they were eavesdropping in on our conversation because every time we would joke with each other or playfully make fun of one another, we heard laughter coming from their table. They'd also say something to each other, then stare over at our table, but we made as if we didn't see. Finally, at the end, all of my friends were like, "Urgh, I'm so full," and I replied, "I'm hungry, I'm eating," and Niall, from his table, joined in and said, "I'm STILL hungry!" At this point we figured it was OK to talk to him since he talked to us first. So I replied, "Well, there are free pancakes at IHOP today!" and he responded, "I know! I just saw that on Twitter!" I also said, "By the way, when you guys are in Boston, there's Wagamama [Niall's favourite restaurant chain] there." His head snapped back towards us, and he said in shock, "There's not?" and Jaki responded that yes, there was, and he looked at Liam and said, "We know where we're eating!" and then high-fived. He thanked us for letting him know, and Liam yet again said he'd see us later.

'Well, we left the hotel to meet up with our friend Marissa. While we were out, Niall tweeted about us, saying, "Someone told me today there's Wagamama in Boston, Can't wait!" so that was pretty awesome. When we got back, Liam came down to the lobby and took pictures with people, so we got pictures as well. We had missed Harry doing the same thing when we went outside for a bit. My friends and I saw all of the boys when they left the hotel to go do press. The ending to a great day was seeing them perform live for the first time as the openers at the Big Time Rush show.'

Tiffani and her friends next met the boys on 1 March; they had gone to Connecticut for the band's tour date and had won a meet and greet. The girls were feeling sad because an announcement had just been made that there had been a death in Zayn's family and he had rushed back to England. They felt so sorry for him. While they were waiting outside a room to meet Harry, Liam, Louis and Niall, the friends heard the boys recording their acoustic set and

were interviewed for the boys' tour documentary.
When they actually spoke to the boys, Niall
remembered that Tiffani had been the one to tell him
about Wagamama and he hugged her.

A couple of days later the girls went to the Kiss108
studio in Boston as the boys were doing an interview
there, but they only managed to chat to Paul. 'The
boys waved at us but it was really rushed there,'
Tiffani explains. 'We checked into our hotel and went
out for the day. We saw the show and when we got
back to our hotel, there was a tour bus parked
outside. My friends and I looked at each other like,
"Seriously?" Our luck was amazing during this tour.
We were at the hotel for two days and saw Liam,
Harry and Louis during those two days.

'We were up late one of the nights and spoke to
Liam for ages at 2 a.m. We asked about stopping for
fans. "We want to!" he explained. "Just sometimes
it's not up to us, whether we want to or not. It's all up
to, like, local police and stuff if we're allowed to stop
or not. If they say we can't stop, we just can't and it's
upsetting for us too."

'He went on to say how he never thought they'd be
where they are and he couldn't believe the kind of
reception they were getting. We told him about seeing
him in Lake Placid and Albany and how we'd never get
that time with him again, and he joked around, saying,

"And yet here we are." We explained it was just dumb luck. He responded that he was sure we'd get lucky and see him again. After about 15 minutes of just chatting, he said goodnight and went to bed. We asked if before they left in the morning he would stop so we could get one last photo with him and he agreed.'

Tiffani and her friends have met the boys so many times that we couldn't include all their meetings in this book. They met Liam in New York on 11 March and, the next day when the boys were performing on *The Today Show*, they were right at the front and Louis held Tiffani's hand as they performed 'More Than This'. When the girls were driving to Fort Lauderdale in June 2012, they pulled over at a service station and found out the boys were at the same one!

'We got out of the car and went to wait in line,' Tiffani says. 'We heard some squealing coming from the convenience store that was attached to the McDonald's, so we got out of line and went to see what the screaming was. We didn't see anything so we went to get back in line. When we got back in line, Josh [their drummer] was in front of us ordering food for the whole bus. A few minutes later, Liam walked in wearing only socks and no shoes. He kept glancing at us a bit as if he was trying to remember where he knew us from. A few seconds later, Louis came running out of nowhere dressed in his pyjamas and jumped on Liam. Poor Liam shouted, "Louis! Dangerous! Dangerous!" as he started to topple over. I chuckled a bit at that. Louis asked, "'Scuse me, do you happen to serve McFlurries at this time of night?" When the woman replied no, he said, "Oh, well, that's unfortunate." He joked with Liam, telling him to order a Whopper as well. My friends and I finally ordered, so we asked our friend Marissa to wait for the food while Jaki and I got us bottled drinks from the convenient store. When we were going up to pay, Liam and Louis were paying as well so we stood back. Liam did a double take at Jaki and me and said, "Hi, girls! How come you haven't come over to say hi yet?" So we looked at each other and said, "Well, you're paying, we didn't want to be rude." The security guard they were with put his hand out as if to block us but then Liam called us over, saying, "No, that's alright! Come chat!" So Jaki and I went over to him. Louis poked his head round Liam and said, "Hi, loves!" Liam asked if we'd been to any shows yet. We told him we were at the show that night, we were going to Fort Lauderdale, and that we had been front row in North Carolina. And this is how the conversation went:

'Liam: "You were front row? I didn't see you."

'Jaki: "Really? 'Cause you were looking right at my camera in a picture I have of you."

'Louis: "I saw you!"'

'Jaki: "Did you really? Or are you just saying that?"'

'Louis: "No, I really saw you!"'

'Me: "Really? Then what was she wearing?"'

'Louis: "Erm, I dunno, something with white in it?"'

'Jaki: "Uh, yeah, actually, I was wearing blue and white."'

'Louis: "See, I know!"'

'Liam: "See, he got this! He got this!"'

'Then the security guard said they had to go. Liam gave us each a hug and said it was great to see us again. As Louis was walking out the door, he said, "Bye, loves!" Unfortunately, we didn't get any photos with the two of them this time around. It just wasn't an appropriate time to even ask for a photo, with Liam not wearing shoes and Louis being in his pyjamas.'

If you would like to follow Tiffani on Twitter, her account is @tiffani_paige.

KRISTEN'S STORY

Kristen is 14 and from Long Island, New York. She met Harry, Zayn, Niall, Louis and Liam at a mall signing on 11 March 2012.

'I waited five hours in the cold to get the album and wristband to meet them,' she explains. 'I got there early but way more people turned up than the organisers had expected. The first 1,000 people were supposed to get a wristband but in the end they extended it to 2,000. My advice for fans hoping to go to a signing is get there really early so you don't miss out. If they hadn't added those extra 1,000 wristbands that day, a lot of fans would have been disappointed.'

KAYLA'S STORY

Kayla is 14 and from Blackstone, Massachusetts. She met the boys on 4 March 2012. Her advice for fans who are trying to get wristbands for an event is to stay in line, even if they say all the wristbands have gone, because you might still get in. When she went to the Natick Mall in Boston, she queued up from 5.30 a.m. and then when she was just five feet away from the front of the queue, she was told there were no wristbands left. 'Nobody moved,' she says. 'Not a single person budged. We waited 20 more minutes until a 1Derful woman came out and announced they were giving out 100 more wristbands. I was number 99. It was so overwhelming. My now BDFFs (Best Directioner Friends Forever) and I stood there and cried tears of joy.'

After meeting the boys and getting their autographs

in her yearbook, Kayla was overcome with emotion. 'Once they gave me my yearbook, I ran,' she confesses. 'I have no clue why. I just flat-out sprinted. Most girls cried but I was so hyped up and had such an adrenaline rush I could've run around the whole mall. And Natick mall is *huge*. All of a sudden, the volume rose so high I thought I was going to go deaf. I later learned that Liam and Louis had asked my best friend Sammy (who was behind me in the line) which drawing she had liked better out of the ones they'd drawn on the table. People had kept picking Louis' but Sammy froze and just pointed at the first one she saw – Liam's. He was so excited he threw his hands up in the air and screamed, "YESSS!" The crowd went wild.'

If you want to follow Kayla on Twitter, her account is @1Band_1Brit_1D.

ANNA LEE'S STORY

Anna Lee is 15 and from Grant, Alabama. She has been a 1D fan since 2010 and her favourite song is 'Moments'. She explains it's 'because it's so deep and personal and raw, like you can hear what's meant to be said and how the boys put their heart and soul into their music'. She wants to be an author one day and currently writes One Direction fan fiction in her spare time. To read one of Anna Lee's fan fictions, search for 'Can't Be Moved' on Wattpad.com. She also sketches and prints amazing pictures of the boys that look just like them. Her sketch of Zayn took approximately three hours for her to draw, shade and add detail. She believes the easiest way to do a drawing is from a photograph, but she can also do it from a video or life. Her advice to fans thinking of sketching the boys is to 'give it a go, you'll really enjoy it and you never know one day you could give it to the boys. They love it when fans give them drawings.' She hasn't managed to give one of her drawings to the boys personally but has posted a few to them. Anna says, 'I have just been offered a place at an exclusive international arts boarding school in Michigan, and my portfolio consisted of lots of drawings of them. I don't think I would have ever realised that I wanted to be an artist without them. They inspire me every day. I hope that maybe one day I could be their very own personal artist.'

If you want to follow Anna Lee on Twitter, her Twitter name is @AnnaLeeMurphyx.

TERIANN'S STORY

Teriann is 16 and from Dallas. She took part in the 'Bring 1D to US' challenges in which US states had to compete with each other to win the chance of meeting the five boys. It lasted four months, and Teriann admits, 'Those challenges drained us all. One involved staying up until 4 a.m. signing "twititions", which affected my grades at school. I was so happy when I found out that my city had won and that the boys would be coming to Dallas on 24 March 2012.'

To get to meet the boys, Teriann had to queue up for a wristband on 13 March. Only 1,000 wristbands were going to be up for grabs but thousands of fans turned up and so 2,000 wristbands were made available. This still wasn't enough though. The security at the shopping mall struggled to control the crowds and the police were called. Six people were treated by the Frisco Fire Department for minor conditions and one person was taken to hospital.

Several fans were interviewed by reporters from TV station CBS DFW. Superfan Gillian Devout told them, 'There was, like, people getting trampled or people on the floor crying, people hurt, people in ambulances.'

Another fan, Taylor Burkhalter, added, 'My friend and I were the first people at the gate. My face got pushed into the wall, slammed into the wall. Falling down on the floor. It was bad.'

Thankfully, Teriann didn't injure herself that day and managed to get a wristband for the event at the Dr Pepper Ball Park. She was blown away by the boys' performance of 'What Makes You Beautiful' and getting to meet them as they signed her copy of *Up All Night* was something she will never forget. The boys loved every moment too, with Liam telling NBC, 'We're just grateful that all our fans showed their support on Twitter and got us over here.'

CHRISTINA'S STORY

Christina is 17 and from Ridgewood, New Jersey. She waited more than 18 hours to see Harry, Niall, Liam, Louis and Zayn in New York. 'After hours of waiting, when the boys finally arrived, it was chaos,' she says. 'When it was finally our turn, all I could do was high-five each of them. I gave each of them a letter on colourful paper in the hope of them reading it and maybe finding me on Twitter. Even though it was only about 61 seconds with them, it was amazing. I'm so grateful that I was given the opportunity and was able to meet them! It's a moment I'll never ever forget!'

If you want to follow Christina on Twitter, her account is @CBones705.

SAMANTHA'S STORY

Samantha is 13 and from Shreveport, Louisiana. She was lucky enough to meet the boys after their

Madison Square Garden show. She wore a T-shirt she'd made with their faces on it and the boys said that they loved it. 'They thought it was so funny,' she recalls. 'It was amazing standing there, having the opportunity to talk to my favourite member, Niall (and the others, of course). Niall's accent is adorable and he is so cute in person.'

HARLEIGH'S STORY

Harleigh is 16 and from Tulsa, Oklahoma. 'When I met 1D, I swear I had a panic attack!' she admits. 'It was at Bring 1D To Me in Dallas, Texas. I cried a lot, but it was worth it! I even met Baby Lux, the boys' stylist's baby at the airport. Lou let me play with her while they checked the baggage stuff.

'I was going down the line to meet the boys and Louis hugged me, he smelled so good! He called me babe, even! Liam and Harry kissed my cheek and told me they loved me; they even followed me on Twitter! Harry was wearing a cream see-through shirt and looked so gorgeous. Then Niall ... Oh, Niall ... he was wearing jeans and a white T-shirt with a red snapback hat. He said he'd marry me, and I asked for a snog. He said yes! We didn't end up snogging but he tweeted me and said, "Love u!" I was crying! Zayn was really nice too, he called me "love" and I touched his hair, he said he loved me as well. He was wearing a white shirt with a funny face drawing on the front. They were really nice and I couldn't ask for a better experience!'

FARAH'S STORY

Farah is 18 and from Queens, New York. She had never been into music until she heard 'What Makes You Beautiful'. A few weeks later she decided to set up a Twitter account and started following One Direction and making friends with other Directioners. She was thrilled when she received a tweet from Zayn saying that she should enjoy school while it lasted.

Her favourite member of the band is Liam, so when she went to see their performance on *The Today Show*, she was thrilled when he waved at her. She couldn't get tickets to their performance at Madison Square Garden but decided to go to their hotel the next day to see if she could see them. She was the first there but soon there were more Directioners and they shared some chips [crisps] Farah had brought with her. She didn't get to see the boys but she saw their pianist Jon and guitarist Dan.

The next day, she decided to go back to the hotel and ended up seeing Niall. He was wearing sunglasses and a beanie, and happily posed for a photo with Farah. She was so happy that she decided to return one more time just in case she could see the others – and she was lucky. 'Day three was my golden day,' she explains. 'After going to buy hot chocolate twice for me and my friends, I heard the boys would be signing autographs at the studio. They were rehearsing for the *Late Show with David Letterman* and I was waiting outside with a friend I'd just made. As the boys came out one by one taking pictures, I took a large breath and repeated to myself, "This isn't a dream."

'I got a picture with four out of five of them and I couldn't have been happier. I had a simple conversation with Louis: "How are you, Louis?" "I'm good, how are you?" I felt my whole life flashing through my eyes. The video diaries, the interviews, and the Twitcams all flashing through my eyes, and I finally was able to prove to myself that sweet and loving boys do exist and they are called One Direction. I just wish all the fans who support the boys, even though they know they don't have a chance to meet them, will get to see these amazing lads! My day of meeting them was unforgettable.'

GREYSON'S STORY

Greyson is 16 and from Allentown, Pennsylvania. She met the boys at their Camden, New Jersey show on 28 May 2012 along with her friend Lana. They had paid hundreds of dollars for two ultimate VIP tickets and arrived at the venue four hours early so they could get a good spot. As soon as the doors opened at 2pm, everyone started pushing, but Greyson was the first inside and so was given the first seat for a sound check, in the front row. She found out that she'd also been given front row for the concert. She couldn't have asked for better seats.

Greyson explains what happened next: 'We all got in line and when everyone was ready, I started to have a panic attack because I thought the girls were going to attack me to get inside, knowing they would be extremely feisty, but security helped me in and I got to sit down first. I was so grateful to the security because I was freaking out so much, and I get horrible panic attacks.

'So when we sat down for sound check, the band [Josh Devine, Sandy Beales, Jon Shone and Dan Richards, who play guitars, keys and drums for 1D] were already on stage and they played us random tunes. Sandy offered me some of the fruits that he was eating and it felt like a mini-party. Honestly, I didn't even feel like a crazy fan, just a friend. So then the boys came out and I FREAKED (but I held it in, I got good at that over the course of the day) and they started to sing covers of a few songs. And then they sang "Moments" and, since Harry was right in front of me, he looked down at me and started singing it to me, and I freaked and cried, since it was my absolute favourite song, and the song was emotional – the only time I cried the whole day! – and he was so perfect … and then he winked!'

Greyson noticed that Liam wasn't wearing any shoes so shouted over to him, 'Liam, where's your shoes?' The music was so loud that Greyson couldn't understand what he was saying but when he came off stage a few minutes later, he explained to her that he had broken his toe. He'd actually broken it by dropping a MacBook Pro on it. Liam chatted to Greyson for quite a while, signing her VIP pass and signing things for other people while he was talking to her. She loved it when he gave her a high-five. She also said hi to Louis and Zayn, but Harry and Niall were talking to girls on the other side of the room so she didn't get a chance to speak to them.

Later on the boys had to do meet and greets and Greyson got to meet them again. 'Everyone was freaking out while I was (weirdly) calm,' she says. 'I was like, "Hey, Liam, how's your toe?" but nobody knew what I was talking about because I was the only one other than the boys and their management who knew he had broken it until he announced it on *The Today Show*, like, two weeks later as "something nobody knows about him".'

Liam told Greyson that it was OK and that he would be wearing shoes for the show. Harry couldn't resist pretending to stomp on his foot. This was one of the best moments of the day for Greyson because they were joking around. She also enjoyed having a hug with Harry and being surrounded by Niall, Zayn, Liam, Louis and Harry when they had a group hug. She loved having her photo taken with them too: 'Harry stood next to me with Zayn on my other side. Harry had his arm around me and squeezed my waist and it was just the best feeling ever. Then when the photo was over, Harry went, "Thanks, babe," and then the meet and greet was over! Ahhhhh, it was amazing.'

When it was time for the concert itself, Greyson was really excited and made sure she had her phone ready to film the boys performing. 'During the first and last song I filmed videos of Harry singing to me and waving. During the entire show my friend was even like, "Why does Harry keep staring at you …?" It was CRAZY, and sounds almost unbelievable. All the boys waved and, during "One Thing", where they throw "snowballs" into the crowd. Liam handed one to me! I also got the chance to have another conversation with Liam while Niall was making a speech. It was an amazing concert and literally the best day of my life.'

You can follow Greyson on Twitter if you like. Her Twitter account is @GreysonAsmus.

CAITLIN'S STORY

Caitlin is 15 and from Charleston. She says of her life before she discovered 1D, 'I used to get bullied big time before I discovered them and now I feel like a girl, and the hateful words slip off my back. Life as a Directioner is amazing! They make me smile more and more every day! They make their fans feel like equals. I truly believe they really do love their fans. They're genuinely sweet boys and I'm here until the end. I'm in love with them, and all their little things.'

LAUREN'S STORY

Lauren is 15 and from Mercer County, New Jersey. She met the boys on 17 March at the *Up All Night* signing at Somerdale's Walmart. To make an entrance, Harry, Niall, Liam, Louis, and Zayn arrived wearing all green because it was St Patrick's Day. They were sat on top of a fire truck and looked down at the 2,000 plus fans that had been waiting for hours to meet them. When the signing officially started, people were moved into the greenhouse area where the boys were. Liam, Louis, Niall, Zayn, and Harry were sitting at a table as they squirted silly string at the fans waiting in line.

Lauren says, 'When it was finally my turn to meet them, I was in shock! I couldn't believe that they were sitting right in front of me! I had written letters to give to the boys about how much they meant to me. When I walked past Liam, I handed him his letter and he winked at me! Then when I approached Louis, I gave him his letter and he said, "Thanks, love" to me! Niall was next but he was very busy signing CDs, so I gave him his letter and he said thanks. I walked over to Zayn and gave him his letter and he said thank you. Harry was last, and my friend and I gave him an icebox, since he had tweeted a few days earlier that he had lost his. I high-fived him and his hand was massive!'

STORM'S STORY

Storm is 17 and from Birmingham, Alabama. She became a huge fan of 1D when her best friend Abigail played her some of their music. They decided to save up lots of money so they could fly to England to try and meet them during their spring break. They did garage sales, babysitting, chores for people, and even got Saturday jobs so they could pay for their airfares. They worked so hard but by the December they realised that were still a long way off raising the money they needed, so had almost given up hope. Then it was announced that 1D would be opening for Big Time Rush in America, so not all was lost! As soon as the tickets went on sale, Storm bought the VIP ones in the hope of meeting them at the meet and greet in Nashville, Tennessee.

On the day of the concert, Abigail's grandparents drove them to Nashville and the girls checked into their hotel as it would be too late for them to go home by the time the concert finished. A short while after arriving, Storm got a call from one of their Twitter friends to say that she had heard the boys were staying at the Sheraton hotel down the road from the arena. Storm takes up the story.

'Abigail and I had to be at the arena by about 3.30 for our meet and greet stuff so we had a couple of hours to spare and decided it was worth heading down there. We threw on our concert attire (dresses and cowboy boots) grabbed our posters, and ran about 10 blocks from our hotel to One Direction's hotel. When we arrived, there were only about 30 girls inside waiting for them. After waiting for an hour, Harry, Liam, Niall, Zayn and Louis started coming out of their rooms and were walking around their floor messing with us and trying to get us excited! Then they finally got in the clear glass elevator, came down and walked past us but they couldn't stop for autographs because they were running late to a radio interview.

'I reached my hand out and touched Louis, and Abigail managed to touch Harry and Louis. As soon as they got into their van, we had to take off running because it was almost 3.30 and we were 10 blocks away. At the meet and greet, we didn't get to meet 1D but we were second row at the concert. I had a poster that said PROM? on it and Niall looked at me and mouthed, "Yeah, I'll go with you!" and gave me a thumbs-up! Later on, during their performance of "What Makes You Beautiful", Harry and Liam sang directly into my camera! It was amazing!'

The second time Storm met 1D was on 25 June 2012. The boys were performing in Atlanta the next night and she had tickets to the concert. Storm and Abigail decided to head to Atlanta a day early to try and find the boys. They searched everywhere and couldn't see any sign of them until they were near a mall in the Buckhead neighbourhood. 'We were walking on the sidewalk towards the mall,' Storm says. 'I had the sense to turn around. When I turned around, I noticed three REALLY big buff men and they all had accents. I told Abigail to slow down and as they got a little closer to us, I could tell that it was Paul, Andy and Preston, the boys' bodyguards.

'Abigail wasn't sure so we played stupid and asked them how to get into the mall, and when they answered us with their accents, we lit up! We were about to walk into the mall when we decided to turn back and ask them if they were One Direction's bodyguards. They smirked and joked around with us and let us take a picture of them.'

The girls tried to follow Paul, Andy and Preston but they lost them. As they were walking, someone told Storm that Harry was at a restaurant, so the girls decided to drive past it. They thought it looked dodgy and that Harry wouldn't be in there. Five minutes later, they found out they were wrong. 'Harry tweeted a picture of the sign of the restaurant and about how he had just finished eating, and I was SO upset!! We could have met Harry Styles!' Storm says.

Later on the girls managed to see Niall for a few seconds. 'We were by a hotel and I heard a bunch of girls screaming,' she remembers. 'I looked up and Niall Horan was in the back of a taxi with his window down. He waved to us and I screamed and freaked out! We went back to the hotel the next day and saw all the boys get into their tour bus and drive off for a radio interview. We decided to head to the arena early and waited for three hours. We saw Eleanor Calder [Louis' girlfriend], Perrie Edwards [Zayn's girlfriend], Louis, Josh Devine [drummer] and

Olly Murs, all from the parking deck of the arena because you could see the tour buses from there. Also, Niall was in the building; he ran across the glass windows and waved to everyone. We met Olly Murs' photographer, who took a picture of us and said he would show it to all of One Direction when he got the chance.'

If you want to see some videos of Storm's experiences, check out her YouTube channel: www.youtube.com/user/ThundaStorm62.

You can also follow her on Twitter: @iKidrauhlStyles.

ELLEN'S STORY

Ellen is 16 and from Los Angeles. She saw the boys on 9 November 2012. Ellen is a huge fan and when she found out the boys would be appearing on the hit chat show *The Ellen Show*, she knew she had to be there. She managed to get an audience ticket and had a blast, watching Ellen ask Harry about his bird tattoos and the boys taking part in a feel-up game with three fans. The fans were blindfolded and had to figure out who was who from the band by just using their hands. Liam was easy to pick out – because of his shaved head.

On her way home with her friends Shelbie and

Sereen, Ellen was feeling peckish so stopped off at an In-N-Out Burger restaurant on Sunset Boulevard. 'We walked in and stood in line,' she reveals. 'I was aimlessly looking at the menu when I heard my friends gasp. I looked up and saw Harry Styles standing there waiting for his food. After it had sunk in, I looked around and realised that Liam, Niall and Andy Samuels [Andy is Liam's best friend] were also there. I did my best to keep calm and, after I ordered, went over and talked to Niall and Liam (Harry had left). It was, hands down, one of the best moments of my life. I never in a million years imagined meeting them, let alone inside of an In-N-Out!'

DARIA'S STORY

Daria is 15 and from Middlesex, New Jersey. She has met Harry, Niall, Zayn, Louis and Liam lots of times. The first time was on 12 March 2012 when the boys were appearing on *The Today Show*. Despite there being hundreds of people there, Daria was one of the lucky few who ended up being seen on TV because of her sign. She explains, 'There was a cameraman in the middle of the crowd in front of us, really high up. When they were showing signs, my friend's sign that I was holding was shown. It said: NOTICE THIS SIGN BECAUSE IT IS DIFFERENT.'

Five days later the boys were doing a signing, but when Daria went to get a wristband for it, she found that there were so many people queuing that they would run out of wristbands before they got to her. Afterwards she looked on eBay for one but they were too expensive. However, she managed to buy one from a fan who was ill and couldn't go.

'Saturday was a blur,' Daria says. 'I remember getting there early and getting in line; it was cold. I talked to so many people around me. It was so much fun. Slowly it got hotter, and I could tell I was getting sick from the sun because that happens a lot to me. Luckily, the boys came soon and we got to go in, and I felt better. I can't even remember what they said to the crowd because I was at standing an angle where I couldn't really see or hear them. I do remember Paul [their tour manager] coming through, and all the cameras everywhere.

'When I went in, I nearly fainted. I'd promised myself I wouldn't scream or cry, so I tried to hold it in. Every time I glimpsed one of them, I couldn't believe it was real. When I was somewhere in the second row, Harry started spraying silly string at the crowd. I yelled, "Harry!" and he looked over at me. I remember going up to the line, and Liam was first. It was all a blur, I don't even remember what happened. I completely blanked out and I still regret it. I couldn't say anything. I remember they all looked so big, and Louis's biceps were huge!'

Daria saw them perform in concert on 25 May but her favourite 1D experience happened on 3 December 2012 at their concert at Madison Square Garden. Daria and her friends decided to move seats to get a better view, so went where there was a big empty section – the security guards didn't see them so they were OK. Daria takes up the story.

'We'd just sat down when Liam's friend Andy walked by. I was the first person to notice him; he looks like a lion. We followed him for a while but then he left. Then we noticed Zayn's girlfriend Perrie. She was in the row right behind us, just a few seats to the side. She wouldn't take pictures but we just kind of stood there next to her. Then Andy came back and he was giving chips to a bunch of people and I realised this might be where friends sit. The row behind us was full of older people.

'Then this man and a girl came and they had the seats we were in, so we had to move. But there were three empty seats and the man said we could stay. I then realised he had an Irish accent and looked exactly like Niall. I didn't know what to do with myself. I just have to say, I have never met anyone nicer and more proud of his son. He asked us if we were excited and we talked with him and asked him the same type of stuff; we couldn't really hear properly as Ed Sheeran was performing right in front of us. We talked about Ed too. Then Ed left and the lights came on. Mr Horan was telling every single person that he was Niall's dad. It was so amazing! He was also pointing out all the family members to us. I can't thank him enough. Everyone else was shying away from pictures and didn't want to be recognised. He was the opposite, and I can't believe we got so lucky.

'We met Anne, Harry's mum, Louis' uncle and aunt, Niall's grandparents, friends and a lot of his distant family. We were talking to Anne when we saw two people walk into our seats and sit down. I realised it was Greg [Niall's brother] and his girlfriend; we had taken their seats, I couldn't believe it. Niall's brother was funny and signed his name huge on my chart. I also got a picture with the Horan clan. We had to go back to our seats though, because the show was starting. The way it worked was that there was a raised platform at the back of the stage. Our seats were as left as you get, and they were perfectly aligned with that platform. Sometimes the boys would go up there and wave straight at our section and us. Niall laughed at us and Harry blew us a kiss. The most amazing part was when I pointed the flash from my camera on us, and Harry waved straight at us, not even our section. I still can't believe it.'

Daria will always remember that night and hopes that one day she will meet Niall's family again because they were lovely. 'I don't only love this band,' she adds, 'but I love all the people I've met and all the experiences I've had. I have a second family now. My best friends are in the "New Jersey Directions Facebook Group" (NJDFBG). We all met online and talked for months before meeting up in person. Now we hang out all the time, whenever we can. We might even be together for New Year's. I love them and everything One Direction has done for me.'

MELISSA'S STORY

Melissa is 17 and from Atlanta, Georgia. She is a member of the group Directioners ATL on Facebook, which started out as a group of approximately 60 girls from around Atlanta. It was set up initially when the very first Bring 1D To US competition launched. Melissa explains, 'We didn't win the contest but we continued the group and started posting anything that had to do with the boys. In the group, there are about eight girls who go to my school, which made me more comfortable getting to know people I just met on the Internet. Now we are all best friends and I don't know what I would do without them. In May 2012, One Direction held an *Up All Night* house party competition. Again, we didn't win, but we held our own and it was the first time we had all met in person. We had a DJ and watched the *Up All Night* tour DVD on a big blow-up screen by the pool. We also set up a Twitter account for the group at @DirectionersATL. At first we didn't think the Twitter would be anything big but now we have over 7,000 followers and a couple of us have been recognised at the mall or in random places. Natalie, another girl from the group, got stopped in a Forever 21 store just last week … it's really weird because people are like, "You guys are so funny," "We love you guys," and we are just like, "Why? We are the weirdest group of people." It makes no sense to me, but oh well.

'When the boys came to Atlanta in June 2012 for their Up All Night Tour, we all got together and spent two entire days running around Atlanta trying to find the boys. The day before the concert, about six of us met Paul and Andy at a Brookstone store in the mall across from the hotel. We decided to go to the hotel afterwards and managed to see Niall and Andy on their way to the mall. Niall gave us a wave but he didn't have time to stop for pictures.

'The next day, we went back to the hotel and saw all the boys before they got into their tour bus. I managed to get a good photo of Niall and Liam. It was a bit manic because there were lots of fans there.

After the boys left, Zayn instagrammed a MacDonald's and some of the girls in our group recognised it so they managed to find the recording studio the boys were going to. I didn't manage to make it there in time due to traffic but a couple of our girls did. They ended up meeting all the boys except Liam and got to go into the recording studio, sound booth and everything. My friend Claire told me after that when the boys came out, Niall went straight to Olivia and hugged her without her saying or doing anything. Getting to hear the stories from Marissa, Tressa, Olivia and Claire really guts me that I missed out but I am so glad they got to meet them! They really deserve it. This makes me all the more determined to meet the boys next year.'

JENNA'S STORY

Jenna is 17 and from Ottawa in Canada but she also met One Direction in New York. She had tickets to see them at the Jingle Ball and had figured out that the boys would be staying at the Trump International Hotel the night before. She thought it would be fun to stay in the same hotel as them. 'The hotel lobby is really small so I thought I would have the best chance of seeing them if I waited there,' Jenna explains. 'So I waited there from 4pm to midnight, just sitting on the couch waiting. I made some friends while sitting there – other Directioners – and it was really nice because I got to know these complete strangers in a hotel lobby all because of One Direction. All of a sudden, at around 8pm, I heard screaming behind me and I turned around and saw so many paparazzi flashes. There was a black van pulled up in front of the entrance, and out walked the boys. I was shaking and so nervous.

'I knew there was a good possibility that the boys wouldn't be able to stop, or they would just ignore us. (There was just me and the other two fans I met waiting in the lobby for them.) The boys walked through the doors and I was trying my best to stay calm and stop shaking because I was in such awe. They were all dressed up in their fancy clothes, with their hair all done up, because they had just come back from filming *David Letterman* and they hadn't changed yet. They looked like proper pop stars. Liam started moonwalking for us, and Louis called us "babe", and it was all so exciting. I didn't have much time, so I took advantage of the opportunity and ran up to Harry to ask for a picture. The security was telling me that he had to go, but Harry didn't listen and he told me to come over to take a picture. I was shaking so much; I couldn't get my camera working and seconds felt like hours. I said sorry because I was taking so long, and he said, "That's alright," and smiled. We took the picture and the boys left to go upstairs.

'I stayed in the lobby in case one of the boys would leave again and sure enough, about half an hour later, Harry came out of the elevator. This time there were a few more people in the lobby so there was more commotion. He stopped to talk to a businessman, took his business card and shook his hand. He was so nice, said hi to people and was very sincere. The next morning I got up early because I knew Harry was out and he would come back to the hotel soon. I waited in the lobby again and, finally, a black car pulled up and out walked Harry. He walked inside the hotel and said good morning to us (me and the girls I met the day before).'

That day Jenna also had the pleasure of hanging out for two hours with Niall's family – his mum, grandma, stepdad and aunt – baby Lux and her dad, Tom Atkin. 'I played with Lux for a bit and she was so cute. She kept taking my phone and pretended to make calls (haha).

'Niall's family was very nice. I was talking to them about everything the boys had been up to lately. Niall's mom, Maura was telling me about how she filmed some bits for the movie with Harry's mom, and that she's looking forward to seeing it when it comes out. I asked her if she had seen the famous One Direction "Mum Song" on YouTube, and she said yes and that she thought it was very funny. At one point, a lady sitting on the couch with us had asked me if I was Niall's cousin, because I was talking to Niall's family and, when I told her I was just a fan, Niall's grandma told me that the fans were very important and their dedication is what got the boys where they are today. It was really sweet of her to say those things, and I'll never forget it.

'At one point, Niall's grandma signed an autograph for a woman who approached her, because her daughter is a big One Direction fan. In the two hours that I spent with his family, we discussed different things from the movie, the Madison Square Garden show, what it's like in Ireland, the general craziness, and the dedication of the fans. They were all so sincere and appreciative of the fan support and were concerned for the girls waiting outside because it was so cold out. What stuck with me that day is how close everyone in the One Direction team is and how nice and lovely they all are. I'm very appreciative of how inclusive they were and the time they spent talking to me when they could have been doing anything else.'

Jenna thought the whole experience was completely worth the travel from Canada.

SARAH'S STORY

When 18-year-old Sarah from New York met One Direction with her cousin Eva, she impressed Zayn with a drawing she had sketched of him. He was being interviewed at the time but noticed the picture Sarah was holding and told her it was 'very good'. Sarah was thrilled and gave it to him to keep. Zayn and the other boys love receiving art from fans and appreciate the time and effort they have taken to create the drawings and paintings.

If you want to follow Sarah on Twitter and see some of her artwork, her Twitter account is @longliveoneD.

JESSIE'S STORY

Jessie is 20 and from Orlando. She met the boys on 30 June 2012 in Orlando, the day of their Tampa concert. Jessie saw them at their hotel and then followed them. 'As me and my friends pulled into the parking lot, we saw this train of, like, 20 cars going around the roundabout and at the front of it was the tour bus!!!' Jessie remembers. 'So naturally, we joined the chain of fan girls' cars following this bus. It was the craziest 30 minutes of my life. Everyone wanted to be next to the bus so they could see Harry eating his banana and waving out the window, but they also wanted to be behind the bus in case it decided to turn at the last minute to try and lose us. So after 30 minutes of chasing this bus through a very busy part of Orlando, we turned off of the main road on to a side street. By this time, we had lost the majority of the girls to red lights and traffic, so at this point there were only eight cars with the bus.

'Then the bus stopped on the side of a small side road. We were all so confused because we didn't think there was anything in this area for them to go to. We didn't know it then but Harry was the only one on the bus. After the bus stopped, one of the security guys got off the bus and told us we needed to leave (sorry, buddy, not going to happen), so we went to pull around the bus and into a parking lot and, as we pulled around the bus, there was Harry, literally hanging out of the bus window trying to get out without being caught by his security. He landed on the ground on both feet and my friend jumped out of the moving car just so she could meet him. As soon as security saw Harry out of the bus, he screamed, "Harry, get back on that bus! Now!" Harry messed around for a couple more seconds then got back on the bus.

'We pulled into the side parking lot with a couple of other cars and waited to see what would happen. The bus backed all the way into a parking lot of a very sketchy [dodgy] strip mall. We were so confused until we realised the very back office of the building was a recording studio. There were about 30 of us waiting across the street from the strip mall because it was private property and only the owner could make us leave. Occasionally, security would come out and tell us the boys wouldn't be able to come meet us because they were too busy, but we didn't care; we just watched the boys run back and forth from the studio to the bus (occasionally shirtless). We slowly began creeping closer and closer to the bus. Mainly to get to some shade. This was June in central Florida, the heat index was probably at least 100°F and we had no water. After two hours, a lady who worked at one of the other businesses in the strip mall came out and asked us what we were doing. We explained to her that we were waiting for One Direction, as they were in a studio a couple offices down. She then invited us into their office to get some water and use the bathroom. She also asked us to send her any pictures we got because her daughter was a big fan, so we got her number, thanked her and went back outside to wait for the boys. In the meantime, the 30 of us spent our time bonding over our love of 1D and many other things that brought us all together: some of us are still friends even now six months later. It was one of the greatest afternoons ever.

AMERICA

The fans waited for about three hours in the Florida heat. 'Andy [one of their bodyguards] came out and told us we needed to go back across the street,' Jessie continues, 'so we did and he came with us. We spent the next 10 minutes talking to him about his life, his new baby boy and what he thought about the boys. He was so nice. He even told us that it was a good thing Paul wasn't there because he never would have let Andy talk with us the way he did. He also said that he really didn't think the boys would be able to come out, so we said that was fine and we all took pictures with him, thinking he was as close as we were going to get. That's when Preston [another of the bodyguards] walked out and said that Niall really wanted to come see us so we just had to be really calm and stay on the sidewalk.

And then Niall walked out of the bus. He looked just as good in person as [in] the pictures, with his Ray-Bans and Captain America shirt. Then he laughed. Oh, geez, that laugh. Everyone talks about how much they love his laugh but you don't really understand it until you hear it in person. He was so great. We talked to him for a little bit then one of my friends decided to be the brave one and asked if we could all get a picture with him. He said, "Yeah! Sure!" So he started at one end of our very organised line and began making his way along, taking pictures and talking with all of us.

After about a minute went by, Harry and Liam started walking our way. It took every ounce of restraint we had to keep from looking like the crazy fan girls we were. We talked to them and then they started taking pictures with us. Liam said, "Oh, geez, I just woke up. I don't know what I look like right now." So he went up to my friend and said, "Hey, can you put your phone on the little front-facing camera so I can see what I look like." He legitimately thought he might not look cute. Is that even possible? So Liam and Harry began making their way through the crowd. Niall finally got to my friends and me. He smelled so I good I just wanted to stand there with his arm around me for the rest of my life ... He also told my friends and me that he wished all fans were as calm as we were. I was so in awe of the whole situation I don't think I did anything other than say hi and smile like a complete freak. Then Liam got to us. He was seriously one of the nicest people I've ever met, he was so down-to-earth, and you never would have thought he was this super-famous pop star. He was carrying a can of Coke, wearing a T-shirt and basketball shorts. I didn't get a picture with Harry but my friend did and she said he was a pretty funny guy. He was wearing a white shirt, black pants rolled up into capris and black Nike trainers.

'After the boys finished taking pictures, Preston said

they had to get back and do some recording, so they all said goodbye and left, and we thanked them. About 30 minutes later, they started getting back into the bus, but not the way you expected. I think it was Louis who started it first: he would get a running start and jump up into the bus from the window, then, of course, Harry, Niall and Liam followed, but Zayn just used the door like a cool kid. Once they were all in the bus, it began pulling out of the parking lot and, just like that, the boys were gone, with a trail of fan girls following.'

CHAPTER TWO

ARGENTINA

One Direction are hugely popular in Argentina. There are over 376,000 Directioners on the One Direction Argentina Facebook page alone, at the time of writing. Harry, Niall, Zayn, Louis and Liam have not visited Argentina yet, but the Argentina fans are just as dedicated as those from other countries.

Superfan Victoria from Buenos Aires says, 'Being a Directioner here in Argentina is weird but great. We love them and we would do whatever it takes to meet them – we are dedicated. We try to catch the boys' attention by contacting them on Twitter and trying to get phrases to trend. They are so popular in my country; their songs are number one all the time on the radio. Everybody is talking about them here.

Many of my friends are Directioners. We have meetings in different parts of the city and we talk for hours about them. We want them to know how much we love them and how important they are to us. We dream that some day they will come to Argentina.'

The majority of Argentina fans can't afford to fly to Mexico or America when the boys are playing concerts over there, so they can only hope that one day the boys will come to their country. The official Argentinian fan club organises a meeting every month so that fans can meet up and make new friends. Lots of fans enter 1D radio competitions in other countries in the hope they will win, but it never happens. Argentina Directioners hope that the boys will do a Latin American tour because there are so many Directioners in the different countries, not only in Mexico where the boys have played.

'Fans in Latin America are completely different from fans from other countries,' Victoria adds. 'We freak out about everything! We would wait outside their hotel during winter or heavy rain, for weeks, if it meant Harry, Louis, Liam, Zayn and Niall would at least wave at us from the balcony. If we had to go, because we couldn't stay any longer outside the hotel, we would write on the hotel walls with messages – our Twitter usernames, phone numbers and stuff like that. I know some Argentina Directioners who, during concerts in the US, have bribed the guards in the stadium so they can sneak in or just to be in the front rows; sometimes it works but sometimes not. If Harry tweets "I'm hungry", I'm sure lots of girls would go to McDonald's and buy them a Big Mac. We get out of control.

'We are really loud. I imagine the boys performing and instead of saying, "WE CAN'T HEAR YOU! SCREAM LOUDER!" they would probably be like, "SHUT UP! WE CAN'T EVEN HEAR OUR OWN VOICES!"

'I think Latin Directioners freak out all the time because the boys won't come to our country, so we don't have the opportunity to see them much. Merchandise here is not easy to find; you can find the CDs easily, but the dolls and the books are not easy to get. We don't have 1D World stores over here, so we have to buy all the merchandise on eBay, which is not good because they never arrive: customs retain all the stuff you buy because they have come from other countries. So the easiest way to get merchandise is when someone you know travels to North America or Europe.'

SOFI'S STORY

Sofi is 16 and from Argentina. When Harry tweeted a photo of the huge screen in Madison Square Garden and announced that they were going to perform there on 3 December 2012, she knew she had to be there. She searched for tickets but they were too expensive. She didn't tell her parents but a few days later, she couldn't help but tell her mother, as her mother caught her crying. Sofi told her that all the tickets had been sold out so there was no chance of her going. Her mother hated to see her so upset, so vowed to try and somehow find her a ticket.

So Sofi went to school but, during the break, her mother called to say that she had found just one ticket, in row 11, section b, which was one of the best sections at Madison Square Garden, at a reasonable price. Sofi couldn't believe it. Her uncle, who lives in New York, found out and he said he would pay for their plane tickets as a birthday present to Sofi. It was only May, so Sofi had a long time to wait.

'Those months passed quickly and it was soon time to go to the airport,' Sofi says. 'I travelled with my mother: we had a 12-hour flight, with a stopover in Peru. I slept like a baby all the way there. When I entered the garden and waited with all those girls, there was this one moment in which the boys' bodyguards appeared and we all started to scream. It was so much fun. The doors were opened, I had my ticket in my hand and the mob was pushing me to the scanner. Many girls went out crying because the scanner said their tickets were not accepted; that was when I started to be nervous. What if my ticket was not accepted, or fake?

'It was my turn and what I didn't want to see showed up: the cross on the scanner. The lady told me to go to window one to check my ticket. I couldn't believe I was one of all those girls whose ticket was not accepted. I thought it was fake, that I would have to return home without seeing the boys, it was horrible. As I was queuing up, I met two girls from Venezuela who had three tickets – two were working but one was not. Their turn came and the guy from the window told them it was OK – to try again in another scanner. When it was my turn, the guy made me wait 20 minutes next to the window because he didn't have a solution to my problem. Many girls had fake tickets and had to buy new ones but, in less than five minutes, there were no more tickets to sell. The guy from the window told me that the stage had been moved forward, so my row had disappeared and that they would give me a new ticket but in a different section. I literally wanted to go home. I'd come all the way from Argentina to see them and they changed my ticket to another section, which I thought was not as good as the one I had. I entered the Garden crying. I found my section ... and realised it was better than the one I'd had! It was row 1 in section 109, which was

ARGENTINA

next to the stage. I was literally two metres away from the stage. In that section sat Andy Samuels, Perrie Edwards and the boys' families – everyone was there!

'The show started with "Up All Night" and Niall waved at me! I was barely breathing. They were so perfect, Harry waved at me and I almost fainted. I was going to throw my phone on stage so the boys could record themselves with my phone or take a selfie, but it ran out of battery, so I grabbed my iPhone case, which was a pink penguin, and wrote "thanks. Sofi" on the inside. I threw it during "One Thing" and Harry grabbed it, playing with it as if it was a toy!'

Sofi and her mother tried to get tickets for the Jingle Bell ball a few days later in New York, and met another girl and her mother who were also from Argentina. A man tried to sell them tickets, saying that he knew One Direction and that he was British, but Sofi didn't fall for it – she could tell that his accent was dodgy. Sofi and her new friend Vicky managed to get tickets from another lady; they made sure that the tickets scanned before giving her any money. They had an amazing time – it was the best week of Sofi's life.

CHAPTER THREE

AUSTRALIA

In October 2011, Harry was asked by *Sugarscape.com* when 1D would be visiting Australia. He told them, 'It's somewhere that we've all always wanted to go, and this whole thing's given us the chance. Hopefully, we'll be there soon and we'll kind of come and say hi to everyone. It's incredibly flattering to know there are people in Australia who are supporting us.'

Six months later, Harry had his wish. He didn't know it then but Australia was to become one of the boys' favourite countries to visit. The first time they went as a band, 300 fans waited for them to arrive at Sydney airport. It was so chaotic at the airport that, for their own safety, they had to leave via a loading dock; this left the fans feeling terribly upset. The boys felt awful and Niall tweeted, 'Australia we're here, sorry we couldn't come out, airport police said it wasn't safe, we really wanted to come out and say hi, cya soon [sic]'. They were taken to the Inter-Continental hotel, where they would be staying for the duration of their visit to Sydney. The boys had the penthouse suite right at the top of the building and, much to the delight of fans below, Zayn appeared without a top on and Liam gave them a wave.

DID YOU KNOW?

Rihanna stayed in the same hotel as them, as she was in Australia to promote her movie *Battleship*. Louis and Zayn actually sneaked out and tried to go to her première without letting their security team know, but it didn't go to plan. Zayn explained to the *Sun*, 'We did sneak away from our hotel at about 8 p.m. – it wasn't like it was 3 o'clock in the morning. But it was a bit like a smash-and-grab – we thought let's go for it! Sadly we didn't really know where we were going and we just kind of wandered around for a bit and got lost.'

On their first day in Australia, the boys went on board a yacht in Sydney Harbour and had lots of fun swimming in the water. The paparazzi took lots of photos of them in their swimming trunks. In the days that followed, Liam and Louis had the opportunity to go surfing a few times, which they really enjoyed. 'When I first started surfing properly that was in Australia,' Louis told *thehothits.com* a few months later. 'So surfing was great there. I just love Australia as a place. Everyone must say that that visits. It's such an amazing place.' He admitted that he would have liked have gone to Australia for a holiday before the tour in 2013 but couldn't because he would have needed at least two weeks off as it's so far away.

DID YOU KNOW?

While Liam was in Australia, his girlfriend at the time, Danielle Peazer, looked after his pet turtles. He admitted during an interview on Australian talk show *The Project* that he had had to split them up because one turtle had bitten off the other one's foot!

Going to Australia with the boys gave Niall the opportunity to spend some time with some of his family who live over there, and he also had a blast with Harry, Liam, Louis and Zayn. After his first day in Australia, Niall told his followers on Twitter: 'See you at sunrise tomorrow, OZ directioners! Off t sleep! Goodnight, great first day down under, gotta good feelin about this trip'.

During their trip, they performed a sell-out show in Sydney, visited Lone Pine Koala Sanctuary in Brisbane, and Niall got to try Vegemite for the first time on the TV show *Sunrise*. Niall didn't like the taste one bit and spat it out on a napkin that Zayn passed to him. After they'd come off air, he tweeted, 'Can clearly say vegemite is horrible! Like tryin' new stuff though'.

The *Sunrise* presenters came up with the idea that they could raise some money for the charity Youngcare if they put Niall's leftovers on eBay. The item's listing read, 'The item is perishable and although we will package it so that tampering is evident, we do not advise that it is consumed. We will not be including the mouthful that Niall spat out – because that's just gross.'

They put the starting bid at $0.99 (64p) and straightaway bids started flying in – in a short time, the bids had reached $1,000 (£648). This was an incredible result, but things didn't stop there – the final bid was an unbelievable $100,000 (£65,000).

It was really hard for the boys to leave Australia after their first visit because they had had such a fantastic time but they'd been missing their families over in the UK and Ireland, so needed to see them asap. On their flight home from Australia in April 2012, Niall didn't feel well, tweeting, 'Not feeling the best! sore all over! under the weather as they say!'

Later on, he tweeted, 'Food poisoning not good!'

Once the boys landed in England, it took them a few days to get used to the 10-hour time difference. They all wanted to chill out and catch up on sleep; they'd had a heavy few weeks.

DID YOU KNOW?

One of the boys' Australian highlights didn't actually take place in Australia!

When Harry, Niall, Liam, Louis and Zayn found out that *X Factor* Australia judge Ronan Keating wanted them to help him choose which groups he should take through to the live shows in the 2012 series, they were speechless. It was a great opportunity and a real honour, as Ronan could have chosen any band or singer in the world to help him.

Ronan chose the boys because he knew they would know exactly how the groups were feeling, and because One Direction are the biggest boyband in the world. Harry, Niall, Liam, Louis and Zayn also prove that a group can succeed after appearing on *The X Factor*. Rather than the boys having to fly over to Australia, Ronan and the groups came to London for the 'home visits' round.

When Ronan introduced One Direction to his groups, the contestants clapped and cheered. They had a quick chat and then it was down to business: one by one, each of the groups had to walk onto the stage and perform one song. Ronan and the boys then discussed what they thought of each performance and then, after all the groups had performed, said who they thought should go through. The boys really liked a good-looking girl group (one of the singers had winked at Harry during their performance) but the groups they decided to put through with Ronan were two boybands and a mixed group: The Collective, who sang Rihanna's 'We Found Love'; Fourtunate, who sang Beyoncé's 'End of Time'; and What About Tonight, who sang 'Gives You Hell' by The All-American Rejects.

Louis told *thehothits.com* afterwards, 'You know what, that *X Factor* experience was actually one of my favourite things that we've done as a band. We did feel a little bit strange to be offering advice; you know we've only been in the game, if you can call it that, for two years. So it was interesting giving advice, but such an honour to be involved in it all.'

The Collective actually made it to the series final but finished in third place, behind runner-up Jason Owen and winner Samantha Jade. One Direction pre-recorded a special performance of 'Little Things' that was shown during the final show.

Getting the opportunity to take their Up All Night tour to Australia and New Zealand in April 2012 was a dream come true for Liam, who had been wanting the tour to go global for a while. He had tweeted months before the dates were announced, 'I want to tour more everywhere all over the world im gunna [sic] miss touring when this one finishes #worldtour'.

The boys' loved their shows in Sydney, Brisbane, Melbourne, Auckland and Wellington. Louis gave a special message to UK and Irish fans in the 1D newsletter, saying, 'G'day! We're sooo excited to have made it to Australia on tour and excited to be in Sydney, Melbourne and now Brisbane. I really enjoyed getting up early to go surfing! So it's got to be said I am LOVING Australia! Missing the food back home though. Big love, Louis :o)X.'

AUSTRALIA

When their 2013 World Tour was announced, Australian and Kiwi fans were excited to see that they had been given more dates: with their first tour, there had only been five dates in total but with the second tour, there were 24!

DID YOU KNOW?

The fourth and final release from 1D's first album *Up All Night* was 'More than This', and it was released first in Australia on 25 May 2012. It premiered on *The Today Show* in Australia. The video simply showed them performing the song on tour. It was released in the UK and America a month later. It reached number 49 in the Australian charts, number 39 in Ireland and number 86 in the UK.

ISABELLA'S STORY

1D superfan Isabella came up with the idea of fans filming their own version of 'One Thing', dressed in similar outfits to Harry, Niall, Liam, Louis and Zayn. She organised and directed the video with her friends playing the band members: her friend Steph playing Harry, Emilie playing Zayn, Eesha playing Louis, Georgie playing Liam and Isabella playing Niall.

More than 20 other fans came along too and the video they made was edited by their friend Jodie. To see the video, search on YouTube for 'One Direction – One Thing Australian Edition'.

TAHNEE'S STORY

Tahnee is 18 and from Sydney. She was one of One Direction's first fans in Australia after she found out about them through Tumblr when they were on *The X Factor*. She loves being an Australian Directioner because, she says, 'We are just so laid back and carefree. We love their music so much.'

Tahnee organised the first ever 1D flash mob and it took place on 21 January 2012 at Circular Quay. A flash mob is a large group of people who suddenly start performing a dance routine in an unexpected place and then quickly disperse. Tahnee explains what happened.

'I came up with the idea of doing the flash mob and suggested it to a couple of people via Twitter to see if anyone was interested in helping me, then I met Mary and Emilie, who became organisers with me. It all started with an idea that was meant to be a joke and we never expected it to turn out the way it did and to attract the amount of attention we received. A hundred fans signed up straight away and said they wanted to take part in the first ever 1D flash mob – I knew then that we had to do it as it would promote One Direction in Australia and hopefully result in the boys visiting Australia for the first time.'

Tahnee created a mix of the *Up All Night* album and, together with her sister, Ashleigh, came up with some dance routines to go with it. She set up dates for everyone to meet up and rehearse – everything had to be really slick on the day or it would look like a mess. The rehearsals took place no matter what the weather: they practised in the rain, in hail and in blistering heat (40 degrees Celsius to be exact!).

'By the date of the actual flash mob, we had about 200 girls turn up,' Tahnee says. 'We went through the routine – amazingly everyone knew what they were doing. It was such an amazing feeling to see something that you have organised actually come to life. Although there was a thunderstorm, we managed to do the flash mob in one piece and the result was pretty awesome.

'The day after we published the video on YouTube, we had over 10,000 views and collectively with another unofficial video, over 30,000 views! We were interviewed by magazines and newspapers, featured on many well-known websites and blogs – and we even got to do a segment on a radio station based on the flash mob for two months. On top of all of that,

Harry spoke about it on Irish radio (Spin), Liam spoke about it on Australian radio (Nova 96.9) and Niall spoke about it in a TV interview with Channel 9's *The Today Show* (Australia), where they previewed our flash mob on live television. And to make things even better, family members and friends of the boys tweeted us about the video, saying they loved it.

'After our video went viral, we began receiving a lot of questions from other fans asking how we did it, if they could use our routine and our music mix. A couple of months and 500,000 views later, flash mobs from other countries began popping up (everywhere from America, Philippines, Brazil, UK, Boston, Canada, Finland, Sweden, Thailand, Greece, Spain, Mexico ... you name the country, they did one!). It was so overly done that the boys' official Wikipedia states, "Directioners are known for doing flash mobs in honour of the One Direction." It's pretty amazing to think we started a phenomenon! It's also great to see fans coming together with just this common interest and become such close friends. In my personal experiences, the girls I have met for the flash mob last year are honestly my best friends to this day. It's amazing to think how this flash mob let me meet so many amazing people and to have the opportunity for all of us to keep in contact.'

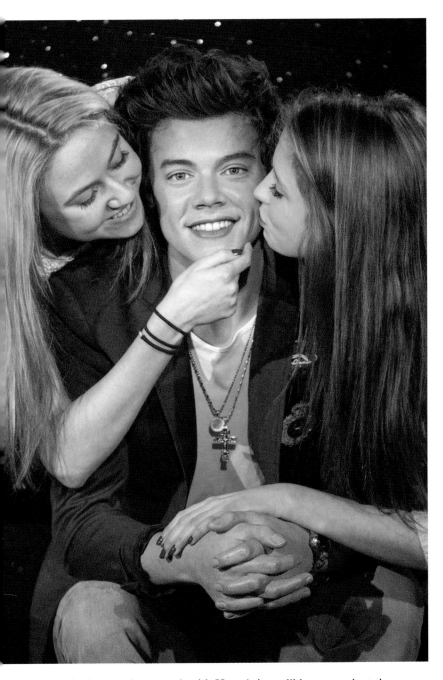

Caption: Lucky fans steal a smooch with Harry's incredible waxwork at the unveiling at Madam Tussauds.

Emotions at the waxwork unveiling ran so high that Tussauds had employ a full-time tissue attendant to help the most overwhelmed visitors!

©Rex Features

Above: Kayla from America chats to other Directioners before she meets the boys.

Below: Harry and Niall high-five fans who have come to their signing in Boston, America.

Above: Victoria and her friends recreate the *Take Me Home* album cover to win the Bring Me to 1D competition in Austria.

Below: Getting hands on: Fans in New York can hardly believe their luck as Harry Styles jumps into the crowd!

Above: The One Direction Mobile. One group of fans in Mexico City make their car a moving shrine to the boys.

Below: Brenna, Miraya, Rebecca and Brigid queue up to see the boys in New Zealand.

The boys always make time to take pictures with fans. Seen here leaving the
Radio 1 studios after a show with Nick Grimshaw.

©Rex Features

Australia's Best Dad Anthony with his One Direction-loving daughter, Catie-Rose.

Above: Cardboard cutout fun in Canada!

©*Rex Features*

Below: Fans in Japan give the boys a welcome not seen since the days of Far East Beatles-mania… Note the band wearing traditional Japanese dress. ©*Rex Features*

A year after the original flash mob, Tahnee and her friends decided to do another flash mob. It was even better than the original – check it out by searching for 'One Direction Sydney Flash Mob Take 2' on YouTube.

MARY'S STORY

Mary is 19 and from Sydney. She has met One Direction three times. Mary co-organised the original flash mob and was staying at the same hotel as One Direction the first time they came to Sydney.

'We'd found out that they were a few floors above us and so we decided to ride the elevator in the hopes of catching a glimpse of them,' she says. 'We'd been floating around the hotel at this point, which was roughly two o'clock in the morning. I'd received a phone call from one of my friends, who was in the lobby telling us to get in the elevator quickly because two of the boys (Harry and Zayn) had arrived back at the hotel after a night out. We did so and we were lucky enough to stop them for a conversation. We asked them about the flash mob and they both recalled watching it and said how much they loved it! At this point, I was completely over the moon with the fact that they actually remembered it and that they really loved it! But the next day we were even MORE fortunate because we got the chance to meet Niall and Liam in the gym. By chance, we went up to the gym and saw them working out in front of the mirrors. We spoke to them briefly and they talked about how thrilled they were to have seen so many fans in Australia when they thought nobody knew them here; both of them loved the flash mob too! It was definitely one amazing experience I will cherish for the rest of my life!'

THE LEE FAMILY STORY

Catie-Rose is 13 and is a huge One Direction fan. She lives in Brisbane, Australia with her mother Colleen, dad Anthony, sister Alice and brothers Henry, Edward, William and Max. Her story starts in November 2008 – before One Direction had even been formed. Catie-Rose's mother was seriously ill and had to have many operations on her brain. Catie-Lee was a big support to her dad and helped look after her brothers. Her little brother Max was only a baby but Catie-Rose would change his nappies and feed him, help around the house and help her brothers with their homework without complaining. She never asked for anything in return, but her dad Anthony promised her that he would repay her one day.

Two years later, Catie-Rose went to her parents and

said that if the band One Direction ever came to Australia, she would love it if they got her tickets to see them. Anthony made it his mission from that day on to do everything in his power to fulfil that wish. As soon as Harry, Niall, Zayn, Louis and Liam announced an Australian tour, Anthony got ready. The day the tickets went on sale he queued for hours and hours but, before he got to the front of the queue, it was announced that the tickets had all sold out. Anthony was devastated when he had to tell Catie-Rose that no tickets were available.

He didn't want to give up, so decided that he would have to try to win some tickets on the radio, where they had One Direction competitions running. He walked around for weeks with his finger on the radio station's redial number so that he could be the first person to ring to win the tickets, but he missed out time and time again. Then a competition was announced asking fans to make a shrine to One Direction, and the winner would be flown to Sydney to attend a rooftop party with the boys. Anthony and Catie-Rose decided to work together and came up with the fantastic idea of having 'shoe boxes' showing the various stages of One Directions growth. They submitted it and waited. Several days passed and, just as they were giving up hope, Anthony got a call from the radio station saying they wanted to speak to Catie-Rose on air!

That night they called and told her that her shrine had made the standby list and she was a finalist. Her whole family burst into tears of joy that finally she might get her wish but, on the night the winner was announced, they found out that Catie-Rose's shrine hadn't been chosen. Anthony and Catie-Rose were devastated, as it had been their last chance to win tickets.

Even though Catie-Rose couldn't see the boys in concert, her family decided to go on a mission with her to track them down when they arrived in Australia. They flew to Sydney with her cousin Maddie and booked into a hotel near to where the boys were staying. All they wanted was for Catie-Rose to catch a glimpse of them but, after four days, they hadn't seen them once.

The Brisbane leg of the One Direction tour came and they were due to perform on the Wednesday night and fly out the next day. Catie-Rose asked her dad if they could go and sit outside their hotel in the car just in case they drove by. Anthony agreed and, after waiting for three hours, the boys' black vans pulled out of the hotel and Anthony, Catie-Rose and Maddie gave chase. Catie-Rose was screaming and screaming that they were so close to them. They followed the black vans through the city to a 'secret' location where a photo shoot was to take place. They saw the boys get out of their van and walk into the building.

They decided to stay put because they knew Harry, Niall, Zayn, Louis and Liam had to come out sooner or later. No other fans had turned up because they had all been on foot and had no idea where the boys were going. Four hours passed and the One Direction minders came out and said that, because there were so few people there, the boys were going to come out and meet them outside. Anthony was overjoyed.

The big moment came and the boys emerged from the building. Harry made a beeline for Catie-Rose and a news reporter stepped in to ask Harry some questions. Catie-Rose held out her iPhone case and Harry asked one of his minders for a pen; he signed Catie-Rose's phone case and interrupted the interview to give Catie-Rose a hug! At this very moment Anthony realised that he had by far fulfilled his promise to Catie, and the emotion of seeing her happiness overwhelmed him and he broke down in tears. The other boys came over to Catie-Rose and Maddie, and also signed her phone case and a sandwich board. Then the boys were whisked away into the waiting vans and that was the end – or so they thought! All the while, the TV news crew were filming Anthony crying and it appeared on the TV news that night. The next morning Catie-Rose's family were watching *The Today Show* (Australia's favourite breakfast TV show) and the clip of Anthony crying came on as the best news story. The hosts of the show said if anyone knew who this dad was, they should contact them straight away. Anthony contacted them and what happened next was truly remarkable.

They rushed the whole family to a location where a film crew were standing by to interview them live on Australian national TV. Anthony told them about his 'journey' with Catie-Rose, how they had tried everything to win tickets and how on the last day they actually got to meet them. The host of the show tried to get Anthony to cry again by saying that they would arrange tickets to the following year's One Direction concert; he didn't cry but later said he came very close. They also said that they have named Anthony 'Australia's Best Dad'.

To see the clip of Anthony crying or to see the family's interview on the news, just Google 'Australia's Best Dad 2012'. You can follow Anthony on Twitter @AnthonyLee59. All five boys follow him and he has more than 70,000 fans. Meeting One Direction has changed the Lee family for ever.

CHAPTER FOUR

AUSTRIA

Although the boys have never visited Austria, there are lots of Directioners there. Fans' messages on Twitter have trended worldwide; they tweeted 'Gotta be Austria' and it was tweeted thousands of times by all the fans in the country because they want 1D to visit them so much. Austrian fans often do joint events with fans from their neighbouring country, Germany. They meet up to discuss the boys, make posters and dance together.

For the Bring Me to 1D contest, Austrian fans had to take a photo of themselves in their favourite place in Austria and mix in something to do with 1D. A thousand fans entered but there could only be one winner – and that was 16-year-old Victoria from

Korneuburg. She made a life-size cardboard phone box with her friends, who would each be playing one of the boys in the photograph. Victoria received a Go1Den ticket, which would take her, a friend and her mum to meet the boys in New York!

Victoria says, 'When I found out about the competition, I thought, "That's my only chance to see my favourite band in the whole world so I really have to win this thing." I recruited my four best friends at school to help me and together we came up with the idea of making a life-size telephone box out of wood, but that was too expensive so we made it out of cardboard. After days of planning, calculating and figuring out who was going to make which part of the telephone box, we had to take the different pieces on the underground in Vienna; people stared at us as if we were aliens. We finally built the telephone box in a small village outside Vienna. Afterwards we took the picture, with us wearing traditional Austrian dresses, which are called Dirlds. We chose to be under/on a tree because we love to be outside. We had lots of fun taking pictures.

'I entered the best photo into the competition and then had to wait weeks before I found out whether I had won. When I got the call saying, "You have won the golden ticket and you are going to fly to New York to see One Direction," I started to scream/jump through the whole flat. I couldn't believe it and my whole body started to shake in shock.

'The hardest thing was that only one friend could come with me and we had all worked so hard on the project together. In the end, the fairest way was to pick a name from random, so Sonja was chosen (she plays Zayn in the picture).'

Victoria and Sonja loved their whole trip to New York but the highlight was obviously getting to spend some time in private with the boys. 'As we walked in, Harry pointed at me and said my name (I know that someone said that there is a Victoria from Austria coming, but still he pointed at me and not Sonja, even though he just heard the name),' Victoria recalls. 'Then I showed them the picture and he said he could remember it and that it was amazing. Harry asked me if I liked the concert … it was just awesome. I even got my book about my BM21D experience signed.

'The only thing I didn't do was hug them. I'm not sure if it was a good thing or not. On the one hand, I think it was good because they have to hug all of their fans and I don't think it's that much fun to hug strangers all the time (especially when you have a girlfriend), and it also meant I had more time to really talk to them. On the other hand, I surely won't have a second chance to get a Horan hug or even touch them. But, anyway, it was just awesome and I loved how Zayn kept smiling at me. I'm proud of myself because I didn't cry and I think it was good for the boys to see a normal girl who just wanted to talk. The whole day was just amazing. They gave us, like, a little private concert and answered a lot of questions. They even answered ours ("What would you do if you could travel in time and where would you go?" – Liam said, "Back to Madison Square Garden," Zayn, "To the future," Harry, "To Egypt to see how the pyramids were built."). In the end we even got to see the new "Kiss You" video, which, by the way, is my favourite.'

To see a video clip of Victoria meeting the boys in New York, search on YouTube for 'One Direction – BM21D – Austria'.

MARTINA'S STORY

Martina is 15 and from Styria. She has been a Directioner for just over a year. She hasn't got a favourite song, she's got 15: 'Moments', 'Everything About You', 'Stole My Heart', 'Taken', 'More Than This', 'Same Mistakes', 'Rock Me', 'Summer Love', 'She's Not Afraid', 'I Would', 'Still The One', 'Heart Attack', 'Little Things', 'Irresistible' and 'I Should've Kissed You'.

Martina explains, 'They have had so much of an

effect on my life. They make me feel loved and happy. I know I am just one of millions of people who love them for who they are but every time I see a picture or a video of them, I am so proud of them and it makes me smile.

'If I ever get the opportunity to meet them, I will say a big thank you to them. I am so grateful for the friendships I have made with other Directioners, because we're a family.'

Martina and her friends took part in a flash mob and hope that one day the boys will visit their beautiful country. The flash mob was held on 10 November 2012 and took part in different parts of Austria, including Vienna, Carinthia, Lower Austria and Tyrol. To see the video just search for 'Live While We're Young Flashmob Austria' on YouTube. The Austrian fans also organised a fan event in Vienna in May 2012 and hope to hold more meetings in the future.

CHAPTER FIVE

BELGIUM

One Direction fans in Belgium have set up their own Facebook page to keep in touch with each other and discuss the latest 1D news. There are currently 1,802 fans on the page and they have a twitter account too. The Belgium Bring Me To 1D competition was really tough – fans had to complete 20 different challenges to get to the final where one winner would be chosen. Some of the challenges included finding a lookalike, designing a 1D cover and dressing a member of your family as one of the boys. The competition was hosted by the Belgium radio station MNM and only devoted 1D fans took part because some of the challenges were really difficult.

Synthia and her friend Kimberley managed to make

it to the final. For one of the challenges, fans had to show their love for 1D on a national scale. Synthia explained on the official One Direction site, 'I ran to the office of Belgian newspaper *Het Nieuwsblad* and begged if there was some way to get me in the newspaper. After some emails, the newspaper published my little "love letter". The same day, I got a call from MNM [saying] that I was selected for the big final!'

Kimberly only made the final after winning the final challenge; fans had to ring up the radio station with the zodiac signs of each member and, thankfully, Kimberley was the fastest. A hundred fans had made it to the final, but after arriving at the radio station, 25 girls were sent home virtually straight away after failing the first challenge.

THE CHALLENGES

1. The coin challenge: Fans had to select an envelope and hope it had a gold coin in it; if it had a silver coin then they were out of the competition.

2. Quiz to test fans knowledge of 1D: This challenge started with easy questions but then the host asked, 'Which month on the official One Direction calendar features a picture of the boys

---

on bicycles?' – only nine fans got it right and made it through.

3. Musical chairs: This was the challenge Synthia found the hardest.

4. Find a volunteer in 15 minutes to sing 'Live While We're Young'.

5. Dress a boy like a member of 1D: Synthia survived this round but Kimberley got knocked out.

6. Guess the song: Synthia knew the right answer straight away – it was 'Up all Night'!

The last round was the hardest round, as Synthia explained to the 1D website: 'It was my mother who had to give the right answer. Her answer was the closest to the right one, so I won the competition! I'm still extremely happy. Of course, I took Kimberly and my mother with me to New York: they both deserved it. We feel very grateful. I think right then at that moment, we were (and still are) the luckiest girls in the world!'

Before Synthia and her mum and Kimberly left for New York they took part in a special show on the radio station so that other Belgium fans could give them some tips on what to wear and what to say. The girls were representing the whole of Belgium and so made sure they took some Belgian flags with them to America.

Their hotel was lovely and they loved receiving the VIP treatment once they got to Madison Square Garden on their second day in New York. 'The hall was huge,' says Synthia 'It was a lot bigger than Het Sportpaleis [the arena in Antwerp] in Belgium, but we were sat at the front, just beside the second stage. While waiting, we spotted Zayn's girlfriend Perrie making her way backstage!'

After watching the boys' friend and support act Ed Sheeran perform, it was time for the boys. 'To our surprise the boys came up on the other stage, the closest to us! It was such an emotional moment seeing them standing so close to us; we let out a few tears of joy! They started with "Up All Night", which was quite special to me because it's the song that made me win the Go1Den Ticket. The boys mostly sang tracks from their first album, but there were some new songs from *Take Me Home*, as well as "Little Things", "Kiss You", "C'mon C'mon".

'The concert was simply amazing; we had the time of our lives! It was so great seeing them in real life for the first time! The guys were just like we knew them from the many concerts we've seen online: they had so much fun, did crazy dances with each other, played games with each other and answered Twitter questions. It's a pity the concert had to end – we wouldn't have minded if it had gone on for ever! Luckily, we'll always have the great memories!'

The girls had a live telephone interview on MNM before going to bed, and they would be meeting Harry, Niall, Liam, Louis and Zayn the next day!

The Bring Me To 1D winners and their guests were taken by boat on a tour around New York before arriving at the secret location. They had to sit at tables and briefly saw the band before the boys went off to wait in another room as fans from every country had the opportunity to see them individually. While they were waiting the winners and their guests got to eat cupcakes, have their nails done and visit a special photo booth. After the winners and their guests had met the boys and had some photos taken, the boys came back into the main room for a Q&A session. The host read out a selection of questions that had been put forward by the winners and their guests (they had had to post them in a special post box in their hotel). The boys had a few more individual sessions with the winners and then performed a private concert. They sang 'Little Things', 'More Than This' and 'What Makes You Beautiful', accompanied by Niall on his guitar. After they'd finished, they said a few last things and said goodbye before walking out of the room.

The host had one more surprise up his sleeves – the winners and their guests got to see the world première of the new 'Kiss You' video. It was great way to end an amazing trip!

MICHELLE'S STORY

Michelle is 15 and from Genk in Belgium. Her dad drove her all the way to Germany with her friend Axana so she could meet the boys at a signing for *Up All Night*. She was devastated when they arrived and found that they were more than 800 girls there, so there was no chance of her getting a wristband. Her dad could see she was upset so told her to search for other Belgian girls who were in the front of the queue and to try to sneak in with them. Michelle did what he said: 'Axana and I started walking. Then there were a lot of girls screaming and running. We thought One Direction had arrived, so we also started running to where the other girls were. Suddenly, we were into the barriers and we were with the first 100 people. The people who were camping there – the first people there – were just trampled. We were crushed into a sea of screaming girls. We might have been near the front but we had to stand for 12 more hours before we would meet the boys. It was really tough; a lot of girls were crying.'

Michelle and Axana received their wristbands at 3.30pm and then met the boys just after 5pm. When they met them on the stage, it was 'pure magic'. Michelle describes what happened: 'When I arrived at Zayn, he spontaneously gave me a high-five! WOW! Then I said, "Hi Harry!" and Harry gave me a high-five! OW YEAHHH! Next was Louis: "Hi Louis!" High-five! BAM! Liam was the same: he gave me a high-five! WHOOOHOOO. Then there was our cute Irish Mullingar boy. I asked, "Niall, can I hug you?" Niall stood up and we almost hugged. Then our magical moment was over because Paul said, "No hug, just high-fives." So I gave a quick high-five to the love of my life.

'When I came off the stage I was still shaking – I'd just met One Direction! Then I realised that I had forgotten my signed *Up All Night* cover. So I went back and grabbed it, but a girl tried to take it off me, saying it was her cover, but it wasn't. I quickly ran to my dad with it before she could take it off me.'

CHAPTER SIX

BRAZIL

Brazil is another country that the boys would love to visit one day but they haven't yet. Brazil's Bring Me To 1D contest was run by the *Fantástico* TV show and to enter fans had to film a video with a parent taking part too. The winner of the golden ticket was 13-year-old Victoria from Cotia, São Paulo. To win her ticket Victoria and her friend choreographed a One Direction routine ... and got Victoria's dad Paul to take part too.

It was actually Paul's idea that they should do a dance routine – and it ended up looking really good, even though he struggled to pick up the choreography at first. They danced to 'What Makes You Beautiful' and 'One Thing'.

It only took them one day to rehearse and then they filmed themselves lots of times until they got it just right. *Fantástico* picked a shortlist of entries and then played them all to Harry, Niall, Liam, Louis and Zayn on 4 November 2012 to see which video they liked the best. The boys liked all the videos but Victoria's caught their eye because of how funny Paul looked doing the dance moves. They told Victoria via the video that Paul helped her to win.

WHY BRAZILIAN FANS LOVE 1D

Mariana, 15, and Julia, 14, from São Carlos first found out about Harry, Niall, Liam, Louis and Zayn when they were searching for a song for their ballet group's choreography. Julia explains, 'We listened to more than 56 different songs, but had almost given up hope that we would find a suitable song when we heard "Moments" by One Direction, and we just fell in love! We used their song and won first place in a local competition!'

Fourteen-year-old Fernanda from Curitiba really admires the way the boys didn't give up when they didn't win *The X Factor*. She also likes how much they care about their fans and always try to make them happy.

Sixteen-year-old Camila from Santana de Parnaíba

became a Directioner when she was going through a really tough time in her life. 'I was moving school, going through family problems and losing people I loved,' she explains. 'I also had problems with myself. I never felt pretty; I used to feel fat and unloved. But then I heard "What Makes You Beautiful" for the first time. The song says that the girl is insecure and she doesn't really know why, and that's exactly what I felt. Being able to listen to the song really helped me and made me stronger. One Direction helped me turn a corner and I am so much happier now.'

Yasmin, 14 years old and from Macaé, is a dedicated Directioner even though her friends at school aren't. She collects any magazines that feature the boys, has posters up in her room and has joined lots of different fan clubs so that she can keep up to date with what the boys are up to.

Rafaela is 17 and she lost a lot of her old friends when she became a Directioner but has gained lots of new ones. She is one of the administrators on the Facebook fan page 'Tudo One Direction' (which means 'Everything One Direction') and it has over 56,000 fans. She says, 'It is difficult for fans from Brazil to get hold of 1D merchandise. To be a true fan is not about having all the magazines, T-shirts, posters, bracelets, books and other things; ultimately, what matters is your love for them.'

Sixteen-year-old Stephani has done some really crazy things since being a Directioner. 'Once I was in school and Liam was doing a twitcam, and I was doing a test,' she says, confessing, 'I left the classroom and locked myself in the bathroom and watched the twitcam. I could have gotten into so much trouble if my teachers had found out.'

MARCELA'S STORY

Marcela is 15 and from São Paulo. She first heard about 1D on 4 November 2010 from her cousin, who called her to tell her about five cute boys who were going to be a worldwide success. As soon as Marcela saw one of their performances on YouTube, she instantly agreed. She explains what happened next: 'The next day I created their very first Brazilian fan site (onedirection.com.br) and in the beginning, it was really hard to find information on them. Because they weren't huge in Brazil yet, my website didn't get many views to start with. I decided to do my best to promote them in Brazil: with my mum, we contacted the biggest Brazilian magazines, radio and television studios. I was only 13 at the time but I wrote to/called all of them to tell them about One Direction.

'I felt so proud when I saw the boys in the biggest Brazilian magazine for teenagers, *Capricho*. It felt amazing. In the months that followed, One Direction's popularity grew worldwide, and the website's views did too. Today I still run the website but I have six more people who help me to update it with translated news, buy stuff to make giveaways, and the best thing, promote meetings for the fans in the two biggest cities in Brazil! It's really nice because there are always a lot of different people united for the same reason, sharing the love that they feel for 1D!

'We were invited to go to an MTV award show, VMB [the Brazilian version of the MTV VMA – Video Music Awards], to go to the stage and accept the award on behalf of One Direction as they could not be there! That was the best experience ever!

'I love all of their songs, but my favourite is "Irresistible" from *Take Me Home*. I just find the lyrics beautiful and I keep wondering if they are singing it for me; lol, just a teenage dream!

'Unfortunately I've never met them, and I don't think they know about the website. This makes me sad, but I have faith that my day will come, as Sony Music Brazil supports us and all the important TV channels and magazines here in Brazil know us, so I just can't wait for them to come to Brazil and make all of us crazy fans happy. You can ask big stars like Justin Bieber, Lady GaGa, Black Eyed Peas, McFly, Demi Lovato and many others what they think about

Brazil and they will say that they love it! All concerts in Brazil have such a good vibe. People sleep in the queue for weeks to see their favourite stars. Most artists take a long time to come but, when they do come, they say they're sorry they didn't come sooner. We have such beautiful places, beaches, people and energy.'

MELISSA'S STORY

Melissa is 14 and from Recife. She started out hating One Direction but is now one of their biggest fans in Brazil. 'It might seem crazy,' she explains, 'but I really did hate One Direction. Someone posted a story about them on my blog with their "One Thing" video and I didn't like it. Then they were in the Top 10 on MTV Brazil and I thought, 'This band isn't funny … they won't be around for long, it's just a fad." I started getting angry about how they were everywhere and then I couldn't get "One Thing" out of my head, it was too catchy. Before long, I was searching on the Internet for their other songs and watching their appearances on *The X Factor*. Instead of finding them irritating, I was falling in love with these five cute boys from the UK and Ireland. Before long, I had succumbed to the "One Direction Infection".

'I set up a 1D fan club on Twitter, started voting for

them to win awards, started watching their shows live on the Internet, even if it was 4am. I made so many good friends who loved them too and I decorated my room with everything 1D related. I introduced my best friend Sarah to them and together we are waiting for the day when they will visit Brazil for the first time.'

CHAPTER SEVEN

CANADA

The boys were supporting Big Time Rush on their first trip to Canada in February 2012 and had a brilliant time. Niall, Harry and Zayn wore blue-and-white Toronto Maple Leafs ice-hockey tops, and Liam and Louis wore Raptors basketball vests for their show at the Air Canada Centre. Harry posted a photo on their Facebook page with the message, 'Do you think we look like tourists in these?! –Harry. x'.

He also tweeted, 'In Canada getting ready to play the ACC! In the Toronto Maple Leafs' Dressing room. We've locked Paul in the toilet'.

All the boys loved their time in Toronto, with Liam writing on Facebook, 'I had the most amazing time last night. You guys were LOUD we could hear every word! Hopefully we can come back and do our own shows soon. Lots of Love Liam x'. He also tweeted, 'Toronto was amazing last night cant wait to do it all again :)'

Louis was a big fan of the food he had sampled, tweeting, 'If anyone wants to eat in toronto go to @loudawgs. Very very good brownie! @loudawgsryerson'.

When One Direction were in Canada in February and March 2012, they didn't stop, doing so many TV and radio interviews, including a great appearance on *MuchMusic* in Toronto. They were also interviewed by Musique Plus in Montreal. They were so grateful to all the fans that came to see them. After leaving Canada, they had to head to Australia, New Zealand and America before flying back to Canada to perform two nights of their Up All Night Tour in Toronto on 29 and 31 May.

Niall said to TV show *ET Canada* presenter Cheryl Hickey during an interview, 'We were just saying last night actually, when we arrived at the airport, we actually really like coming to Canada, there's such a good vibe around.'

On the day of their final concert in Canada, they were interviewed by *MuchMusic* again, and asked how they were going to stay sane with more than 100 tour dates in 2013. Harry told the host Lauren

Toyota, 'It's nice for us to bring our friends sometimes out with us on tour, and family members and stuff, it's nice for us to kinda have people to hang around with as well as each other.'

The boys admitted that on their days off they like to have lie-ins, play video games and go sightseeing. They find that once they have left their hotels (and the fans waiting outside) they can have a pretty normal day – but they do sometimes have to sneak through the kitchens in restaurants to escape if too many people are following them.

DID YOU KNOW?

The boys favourite Canadian is Michael Bublé. Niall told *ET Canada*, 'I think he's just such a natural performer, he's got a great voice, he looks good ... he's a really, really nice guy.'

YTV Canadian cable channel were given the task of finding the Canadian Bring Me to 1D winner and so invited fans to submit a one-minute video saying why they should win the title of One Direction's number-one Canadian fan. They were bombarded with more than 24,000 videos!

After watching all the videos, they created a shortlist and then picked the fan they felt deserved the award the most, 17-year-old Amanda from Nepean, Ontario. Amanda actually filmed the video with her identical twin sister Brittany (of course, she picked Brittany to go to New York as her special guest!). The girls found out they had won when they arrived home after volleyball practice to find Carlos, the presenter of YTV's *The Zone* in their kitchen. To see their winning video, go to YouTube and type in 'Canada Loves One Direction – Please Bring Me To 1D, YTV!'

The girls took lots of videos during their special day with 1D in New York and uploaded them on their YouTube channel 'CanadaLovesOneD'. They also set up one of Canada's first Tumblr accounts, canadalovesonedirection.tumblr.com, and received a letter from the boys' management company thanking them for helping promote the boys in Canada.

VANESSA'S STORY

Vanessa is 16 and from Toronto. She met One Direction on 30 May 2012. The boys don't come to Toronto very often so, when she found out they would be spending their day off in the town, she decided to try and find them along with her friends Amanda, Celine and Amira.

'We literally looked all over Toronto to try to find them (looking in loads of Starbucks),' she remembers.

'And when we got to their hotel, the Ritz Carlton hotel, we were relieved that there weren't many people. We waited for a little bit but decided to just keep searching around because why would they stay in their hotel on their day off? As we were crossing the street, we spotted Louis and his girlfriend Eleanor just walking around. We went up to them very calmly and they were honestly so sweet to us. There were only five of us so we all got to chat with him for a couple of minutes. He is honestly the sweetest person ever. He didn't need to stop for us but he did. We weren't allowed pictures but we didn't complain because we ended up in a paparazzi one, which was posted online and in magazines. (As they are walking, you can see me in the middle of them in the background.)

'Meeting Louis literally meant the world to me. I had so many emotions running through me and till this day I still can't believe that I got to meet him. After we met him, we kept walking and saw the boys' tour bus in the parking garage. We talked to the security and, of course, they tried to convince us that the boys weren't there, but we knew they were. So we waited and, finally, the tour bus was coming out, but they didn't stop. We still got them all to look out of the windows and wave, which was amazing. We ended up chasing the tour bus until they were near the highway (oops). Every single time the bus stopped, we stopped and, every once in a while, Harry would stick his head out and tease us (he's so cute, I'm so in love). They were going to Niagara Falls.

If you want to follow Vanessa on Twitter, her Twitter name is @nippleshire.

KRYSTLE'S STORY

Krystle is 20 and from Mississauga, Ontario. She met the boys in March 2012 when they flew into Toronto Pearson International Airport. They had flown there to be on a hit Canadian YTV show called *One 2 One*. They were going to sing a few songs and be interviewed too. Krystle would have given anything to be in the audience but she couldn't because the only way to be in the audience was to have connections or to win a radio contest on Kiss92.5. She had entered the radio contests but failed to win.

Krystle and her friend Lucas could have waited outside the TV studios but they figured they would have more chance if they went to the airport and saw the boys arrive. Krystle explains, 'I went with my friend Lucas and we arrived at the airport at around 11am. We decided to go early so we could look for back doors and other places the boys might come out of. We decided to be there for each and every flight just to make sure we wouldn't miss the boys. As we waited for the very last flight at about 10pm there were about 12 fans and two paps [paparazzi] waiting by us. The pap standing next to the side door shouted, "Now!" and then the doors opened and Harry walked through first, followed by Zayn, Niall, Liam and Louis. Harry looked as if he wanted to walk over towards us but his security team would not let him. I was the first to speak and I said, "Hi, Zayn, I love you, can I have a picture?" Zayn smiled. Paul, their bodyguard, said, "Walk with us," which is what we all did. We gave them a huge amount of space between us and let them walk ahead. Will Wong, a celebrity blogger from Toronto, jumped in and he got a photo with Harry.

'I loved being able to talk to Harry and I asked him to sign my CD. He said, "Sure," but was pushed out the doors by security and right into their waiting car. The boys looked really upset as Niall shook his head and didn't know what to do. I may not have gotten a picture with the boys but I saw them two feet in front of me and that made me so happy.'

GILLIAN'S STORY

Gillian is 19 and from Vancouver. She met the boys on 8 November 2012. Gillian had heard that Harry, Liam, Louis, Niall and Zayn would be performing on the *The Ellen Show* in Burbank, California, and really wanted to be there, even though it was over 1,000 miles away. She requested tickets on *The Ellen Show* website a week before their performance and a couple of days later received an email saying that she had two 'stand-by' tickets. This meant that Gillian and her friend Holly might not get to go in; it all depended on how many people turned up. Gillian was determined to go and booked flights for the two them.

'My aunt lives in the Los Angeles County,' she recounts, 'so we stayed there for the weekend and we were able to borrow the car to get to the show. I didn't miss many classes because luckily this was during the Remembrance Day long weekend. In the email I received, we were told not to show up at the designated check-in place before 10am, but we wanted to play it safe, so we showed up at 8.30am. We weren't completely surprised that a massive line had already formed when we arrived. The *Ellen* staff started letting people through around 1pm. *Thankfully*, we got let through! Or else that trip would have been a waste. The fans we met in the line were great. They didn't believe we'd travelled all the way from Canada – they even asked us to show them our IDs. Finally, we got our wristbands and were ushered in the charter buses that took us to the Warner Bros Studios (the check-in place wasn't where the boys actually performed). There were around 5,000 people in the audience and they had an outdoor stage set up for the boys' performance. When we got there, the staff were keeping the audience entertained by playing music while the remaining people arrived. Before the show was about to start, my friend and I were leaving to go find a washroom but, as we were leaving, everybody started screaming! I turned around and there was Harry – in the flesh! The rest of the boys followed suit. The audience went wild; it was bizarre. I was caught off guard and I wasn't prepared so all I could do was smile. I started laughing because I couldn't believe what I was seeing.'

SIBEL'S STORY

Sibel is 16 and lives in Toronto, Ontario. She will never forget the day she logged into her Twitter account and found out that all of the boys from One Direction were following her. It was Friday, 23 March 2012 and Sibel had just got in from school. She was so excited that she started crying. All Directioners on Twitter dream of the 1D boys following them, so Sibel was over the moon to have all of them follow her on the same day. She loves all of the boys equally; however, if she were to choose her favourite, she would have to go with Niall.

A few hours later, Sibel checked her Twitter mentions and was surprised to read a tweet from someone saying, 'Hello, I am the executive producer at *MuchMusic*, please follow me so that I can DM you.' *MuchMusic* is a hugely popular music channel in Canada, but Sibel couldn't understand why someone who worked there would want to get in touch with her.

She followed him anyway, and he quickly replied in a direct message saying, '*MuchMusic* is shooting a pilot TV show this Monday 1.15pm on superfans. You have to be at least 14 years old to participate. Interested?'

Sibel quickly replied, 'Yes'. Of course she would be there!

He replied, 'OK. You and your sister need to be at *MuchMusic* at 1.15pm this Monday. On the John Street entrance. Have you been to *Much* before? Also, we need to keep all TV pilots confidential until they get fully completed.'

Sibel knew that the boys were supposed to be in Toronto that day but she didn't think they would be at *MuchMusic* because the producer would have told her if they were – but she figured that being with other superfans would be cool. She found it so hard to keep the fact that she was going to a TV pilot a secret, only telling her sister and parents.

The day finally arrived and Sibel decided to get up at 7am. She had hours until she had to be at the TV studio but she was going to go into town early with her sister Melike to see if they could see the boys at their hotel. It had taken them three hours in freezing weather to get there and it got a bit much for Sibel, who started to cry (they'd actually gone to the wrong hotel). She really wanted to see Harry, Liam, Louis, Niall and Zayn so much, even if it was just for a second, but there was no sign of them.

Sibel was still feeling emotional when they arrived at *MuchMusic* and saw the other 20 or so Directioners who were gathered there. No one had any idea what was going on but they were quickly ushered inside and their coats and belongings were taken off them. Sibel was called over to one side and taken into another room (along with her sister). Inside was the producer who had tweeted her and he said it was nice to meet her and asked her a few questions. He then took them onto the stage and Sibel was handed a microphone to attach to her shirt. She was one of only three fans who was going to be interviewed by the host, Lauren Toyota.

When the filming started, Sibel was so nervous and thought she was speaking really fast when she was asked questions but, if you watch the video yourself on YouTube, you won't be able to tell. Just search

'One Direction Revealed – *MuchMusic*'. All the girls were really excited to be there and screamed when the host said, 'We have a person who's experienced being a Directioner,'– and the boys popped up on a TV screen that had been set up close by. They couldn't believe One Direction were Skyping with them but, before Liam had chance to speak, the screen went black: the boys had been cut off. Sibel was devastated, yelling, 'Noooo, my babies are gone!' She'd forgotten they were being filmed. Lauren told them that they were having technical difficulties and two minutes later the lights in the room started going on and off. Sibel didn't know what was happening, but then she looked to the left with the rest of the girls when a curtain fell, and saw Harry, Niall, Liam, Louis and Zayn in the flesh. The boys were in the studio with them!

Sibel started screaming and freaking out, so excited that she nearly fell on the floor with shock. The other girls were just as hyped, so Liam told them, 'Slow down, girls! You guys are going to get hurt! Let us come to you!' The girls went back to the spots they had been given and Sibel was right at the front by the couch. Sibel felt like pinching herself when Lauren told the three of them to move behind the boys – she got a huge hug from Harry. They hugged each other so tight that Sibel says it was by far the highlight of her life.

'That hug was so intense,' she explains. 'I was like, "I Love You!" and he hugged me tighter, and then he was like, "Are you OK, babe?" and I was like, "Noooo," and he kind of giggled, but we were still hugging. I whispered in his ear, "Harry, can I have a kiss on the cheek?" and he was like, "Of course, babe," and then, while he was still hugging me, he turned his face round and kissed me on the cheek. And then I kissed him back on his cheek and then had to let him go. It was amazing. Harry gives the best hugs in the whole entire world and his cheeks and lips are so soft.'

Harry and the other boys were then going to be interviewed by Lauren, with Sibel standing a centimetre behind Harry and Zayn. Before the interviewed started, Sibel had the opportunity to quickly speak to Zayn and asked him, 'Do you remember me from the email? You followed me on Tuesday!' and he replied, 'Yeah, I remember you, babe!' In the email, she had asked if she could meet them while they were in Toronto; however, they had told her that the boys would be too busy to meet fans while they were there. Zayn knew how big a fan Sibel was because he'd watched her being interviewed earlier too in a backstage room.

During the interview, there was a scene involving a cake and Liam gave Sibel the biggest smile when she yelled, 'Cookie Man!' [In a Twitcam Liam did on the 15th March 2012 he introduced 'The Cookie Man', as he received cookies and a drink from room service.] She also made Louis laugh and Niall giggle when she told a joke. Zayn's hands got covered in cake, so he asked for a tissue and Sibel couldn't resist whispering cheekily, 'I'd lick it off you.' Zayn looked at her and smiled.

When it was time for the boys to go, their security team told the girls that there was no time for hugs but Sibel asked Niall for one quick hug and he did – he always puts fans first. Sibel was so happy and waved to Zayn as they were walking out, saying, 'Bye, Zayn!' She was so shocked when he came back and took her hand and held it, saying, 'Bye, babe.' It was better than she had ever dreamed.

If you would like to follow Sibel on Twitter, her account is @ILouv1Direction.

CHAPTER EIGHT

CHILE

Chilean Directioners had to find secret codes and put them into an application in order to win a Go1Den Ticket. The winner was Florence, who had spent two weeks listening to the Top 40 Chile radio station, and going on the social networks of the radio station and Sony Music Chile. Florence was invited to the Go1Den Ticket offices at Sony Music Chile to collect her huge ticket – she couldn't have been happier. There are over 130,000 Chilean Directioners on the One Direction Chile page on Facebook alone, so Florence had been up against lots of fans who all wanted to win the trip to New York.

In March 2013, some of the Chilean fans travelled all the way to the UK to see the boys perform in Liverpool. A fan called Denisse posted up photos and updates so that all the Chilean fans could experience what she was seeing. One of the photos showed Liam lifting up Harry's shirt and revealing the butterfly tattoo on his chest.

One Direction Detection Chile is a fan club representing all the Directioners in Chile. The club is run by Ann, Melanie, Paloma, Gabriel, Ale, Javiera and Daniela. They are really passionate about Harry, Niall, Liam, Louis and Zayn, and have organised lots of get-togethers for fans to meet up and talk about the boys. On 23 July 2012, they met up to celebrate the second anniversary of One Direction and had a big party. They even had a 1D cake. For Liam's 19th birthday, hundreds of Chilean Directioners got together to wish him a happy birthday through a special video. They celebrate all the boys' birthdays but Liam's was the first they did that involved a video. To see the video, go to YouTube and search for 'Happy 19 Birthday Liam Payne From Chile'.

Here are some messages Chilean fans from the fan club want to give to the boys if they ever come to Chile:

'THANK YOU for everything. You help a lot of people with low self-esteem and it is really admirable.' Constanza

'I'm grateful for what you have done for us, personally. One Direction have helped me in many ways. Hope to see you soon in Chile, kisses.' Franceska

'Thank you for being my smile every day, thanks for making me feel pretty, special and unique, thanks for your dedication to your fans. I love you so much.' Montserrat

'I want to thank them for changing my life and for teaching me to not lose hope and to fight for my dreams.' Sofía

'They are part of my daily life, part of my life, part of me. They bring happiness to a lot of people and I'm so proud to be a Directioner, they make every day special.' Diego

CHAPTER NINE

CROATIA

Sadly, Crotian Directioners didn't get a chance to enter the Take Me To 1D competition but they hope that they will be able to enter other competitions in the future. Superfan Petra Styles created a great video for YouTube, which sums up how Croatian fans like herself feel. The text accompanying the images she has chosen reads:

'Dear One Direction, you are more than just "that boy band". You're more than just "five hot guys", you're more than "the boys who almost won a TV music competition", you're more than what people think you are, you're a big inspiration, a motivation and a dedication, in you, we see what people don't see, we see talent, courage, power and hope. In you

127

we see the most beautiful unbreakable friendship, you're proof that dreams do come true. You make us realise that even if you are just a small town person you can become that big time sensation. You make us cry, laugh and, most importantly, you make us realise that it is okay to be yourself.'

At the end of Petra's video are photographs of Croatian fans asking 1D to visit their country.

GABRIELA'S STORY

Gabriela is 15 and from Zagreb. She says, 'There are 40,000 Directioners in Croatia. In June 2011 Liam noticed Croatia and tweeted "LP loves Croatia". That was the beginning of everything. Since "What Makes You Beautiful" and their album *Up All Night* came out, their popularity has just grown and grown. *Up All Night* became number one, but the boys didn't visit Croatia. The media started reporting One Direction news every day, on TV, radio, magazines. I think Croatian Directioners are different to Directioners in other countries; our specialty is that we're crazy and creative. There are also lots of boy and adult fans.

'Our biggest dream is to have a chance to hear and see them live and thank them for everything. It's impossible to not know about them. They're everywhere here in Croatia. All the people know how much we tried to bring 1D here and they say that they're proud of us. It's nice to be a Croatian Directioner because we're full of power, love, faith and hope. We hope that one day we will be so happy that our biggest dreams will come true.'

Gabriela and her friend Asja run the Official 1D Street Team (follow them on Twitter @1DTeamCRO). They have held many 1D events. In April 2012, they made a big *Bring 1D To Croatia* video. It had almost 20,000 views and appeared on all major Croatian sites, on TV, on the news and on the Croatian celebrity programme *Exkluziv Tabloid*!

And that wasn't all. In July 2012 they organised a 1D summer fan meeting and two months later they organised a BIG 1D fan meeting and a 1D flash mob. This was shown on TV and the boys themselves got to see it. At Christmas they organised another fan meeting, which was shown on TV.

Gabriela is so proud of Croatian Directioners and the work they have done to try and get Liam, Louis, Niall, Zayn and Harry to visit them. She is proud of the boys too because to get *Up All Night* and *Take Me Home* to number one is a huge achievement as 'it's hard to be number one here'. She thinks, 'if they ever came here, their concert would be the biggest ever!'

CHAPTER TEN
DENMARK

The One Direction Denmark Facebook page is run by Faidao, Fie and Narin and it has 169,000 fans. The girls encourage fans to share positive posts about the boys and to ignore the haters who post negative messages.

Danish fans were so excited when they found out the boys would be performing at the Jyske Bank Boxen in Herning on 5 May 2013 and at the Forum Stadium in Copenhagen on 10 May as part of their World Tour. It would be the first time the boys had ever been to Denmark. Superfan Caroline from Copenhagen got her parents to buy her tickets for the 5 May concert as soon as they came out. Most Danish fans discovered One Direction when they released

'What Make You Beautiful'. Caroline and her school friends loved watching the video on YouTube; Caroline liked Harry the most but her friends all thought Zayn was the hottest.

Caroline says, 'My favourite song at the moment is probably "Loved You First" because I know the feeling of loving someone "first" and then seeing them getting together with someone else – I mean, isn't that what all fans go through?

'There was a Danish fan event in a little town called Taastrup and it was really great. I went with my best friend Emilie, who I met because we both loved One Direction. They played the new album, we saw the Up All Night Tour and there was a competition where we could win a message to the boys and concert tickets.'

Lotte, 15, from Vekso, loves being a Danish Directioner too, and says, 'Being a fan in my country is pretty great, I think. One Direction knows where Denmark is and their vocal coach is from Denmark, so that is really cool, I think. And they are coming here on their tour. Also, there are really many Directioners in Denmark. So you are not "alone" and that is great.'

The Danish winner of a Go1Den ticket was Nanna and she took her friend Linea with her. Nanna created a really funny cartoon telling the fictional story of what happened when 1D visited Denmark for the first time. Nanna acted as their guide, taking them around the big Danish landmarks, but then the boys all got bored (apart from Liam) so Nanna showed them the fun things people in Denmark like to do – like visit Legoland (with Ed Sheeran), go swimming (Harry stripped off) and eat Danish food (Niall loved this one). Zayn even got a Danish makeover. To see the video, just search on YouTube for 'Winner of Bring me to 1D Denmark – Linea & Nanna'. At the end of a video they posted of themselves meeting the boys, a message reads, 'Huge thank you to everybody who has made this experience possible for us! And thank you to the boys for giving us an amazing and memorable year! Love from Denmark.'

When Linea is older, she wants to work in animation. Her profile on YouTube states, 'I LOVE LOVE LOVE to draw and I am dreaming of becoming an artist in animation, travelling the world and work with talented artist all around the world!'

CHAPTER ELEVEN

ECUADOR

The boys might have been to many countries around the world but they have never been to Ecuador, so fans in the country have been campaigning and doing flash mobs in the hope that they can encourage One Direction and their management to visit one day. In one of Liam's twitcam's he said, 'Hi Ecuador! Hello', which meant a lot to the fans who had stayed up late to watch it live.

MELANIE'S STORY

Melanie is 17 and from Guayaquil. Melanie didn't want to have to wait until the boys decided to visit Ecuador before seeing them, so travelled all the way to Fort Lauderdale in Florida to see Harry, Niall, Louis, Liam and Zayn in concert. The flight alone took four hours. Melanie and her family arrived a few days early, so Melanie tried to find out where the boys were staying. She thought they would be staying at the W hotel and figured out how long it would take them to drive from their concert in Orlando to the hotel. 'At around 9pm I went for a drive with my parents around the city in case we could see their tour van,' she says. 'We were on our way back to our hotel at around 1.30am so I asked my dad if he could drive to the W hotel just to find out if they were arriving there or not.

'Around 2.10am we arrived and there was not any sign of them being there. I was very disappointed but on our way back to our hotel my dad spotted their tour vans outside another hotel. We parked up and went inside the hotel but then we were told the boys were still outside. My dad tried to step into their tour bus but security kicked him out. No other fans were there so I felt really blessed.

'I met Zayn and his best friend Danny and then I said, "Hola, Niall," because I knew Niall speaks a little bit of Spanish. He turned around, smiled at me and said, "Hi." I then told him that I had come all the way from Ecuador just for their concert and he made, like, a surprised face and said, "See you tomorrow then."'

The boys were really tired and had to go to bed but Melanie didn't mind. She enjoyed chatting to their security guard Paul and even had a photo taken with him. She was so thrilled that, even when she went back to her hotel room, she couldn't sleep until 5am.

PAULA'S STORY

Paula is 17 and is also from Guayaquil. She met the boys when they were in New York to promote *Up All Night*, as she was there on holiday at the time. She knew the boys were staying in Manhattan and managed to convince her mum to help her track them down. She had heard a rumour about which hotel they were staying in, so together they went to 54th Street and, sure enough, found the hotel with 20 or so fans waiting outside. After waiting for nearly two hours, Harry came out and jumped in a waiting car. Paula's mum wanted to go shopping so Paula had to leave but they came back later that night.

Paula says, 'The second time, there were more girls and it was freezing cold. I overheard a girl say that the boys were coming out soon, so decided to follow her behind the hotel. Seconds later a car appeared out of the garage and the five boys were all in there. Me and the other girls start running behind the car like maniacs, and that's when the car hit a red light. I knew it was my chance, so I tapped on the window and waved at Louis who was looking straight at me. He smiled and put his hand on the car's window and I put mine on it too so it looked like we were touching hands. I saw Zayn was laughing in the background, but then the lights changed and the car took off. I wasn't fast enough to catch up with it again.'

Paula didn't think she'd see them again but her mum agreed that they could go back the next day, as the boys would be leaving for Dallas really early. Paula managed to see her favourite member of the band, Harry. 'I waved at him and he waved back with his cheeky smile,' she remembers. 'I start screaming in my head as my celebrity crush had just waved back to me. I was there for about five minutes with security trying to block my view of Harry but I managed to still film him. He rolled his window down and waved to some fans beside me; he's, like, the sweetest boy ever.'

Paula wishes the boys would come to Ecuador one day but, until they do, she will make more trips to the USA when they are there. She loved seeing them perform their Take Me Home concert in June in Miami. It was the best concert she had ever seen.

CHAPTER TWELVE

FRANCE

Harry had been to France when he was at Holmes Chapel Comprehensive School on a school trip, but the first time he went to the country with a member of One Direction was in April 2011, just after *The X Factor* tour had finished. Harry and Louis decided to go skiing in Courchevel, France together because they knew they would be really busy in the months that followed and wouldn't have time for a holiday. They took two of their friends with them and had a blast. Harry had never skied before so fancied giving it a go.

While they were there, a couple of fans spotted them and tweeted, '16/04/2011 proud to say I met @louis_tomlinson and @ harry_styles in a bowling alley in courcheval' and 'I met you in courchevel. Best day of my life'.

The paparazzi didn't expect them to go on a skiing holiday and the boys kept where they were going a secret from the press. If they'd gone somewhere hot, they probably would have been followed. Two photos did appear on Twitter though – one of them wearing their skis and the other of Harry with a fan on the slopes. Harry really enjoyed himself and in December 2012, he went skiing in Utah, USA with his girlfriend at the time, Taylor Swift. He ended up hurting his chin though, and had to wear a bandage on it over Christmas.

DID YOU KNOW?

During his first ski trip with Louis, Harry wore orange trousers and, during his trip with Taylor, he wore an orange hat. Harry loves orange!

The boys spent Valentine's Day 2012 in Paris as they were in France promoting 'One Thing'. They had lots of interviews in the daytime and then in the evening they went out for a meal together. They might have had an unromantic Valentine's Day but they still enjoyed themselves. Harry tweeted, 'Happy Valentine's Day!!! We couldn't do this if it wasn't for you and we love you for that. Hope everyone has a lovely day! Oui Oui!!. Xx'.

Niall told his followers, 'Happy Valentine's day everyone, love you all so much. if it wasnt for you there would be no 1D'.

During their stay, Niall tried to speak in French to any fans and interviewers they met because he'd loved his French classes at school. He'd never been to France before, so it was the first time he could show off his skills in a real setting.

If One Direction superfan Francia had to describe French Directioners in two words, she would say 'dedicated' and 'crazy'. 'Every time they come to Paris, thousands of girls come to see them, even if it is just to see them for a few seconds,' she says. 'I know because I am one of those girls. I have witnessed girls crying because they didn't get to see them and sometimes it is heartbreaking.

'A lot of French Directioners travel over to England to see them perform in concerts over there. We also do different projects to show Harry, Niall, Liam, Louis and Zayn how much we support them. We did a flash mob in front of the Eiffel Tower and it was shown on television. We also meet up to socialise. French Directioners made a really strong impression on the boys when they came to Paris for the second time because it rapidly turned into madness, and Liam even lost a shoe! I think that was the time when the boys realised their impact overseas. Because of that, we are often considered very crazy and excitable.

'I can't really tell what difference there is between French fans and the others, but perhaps their interviews in our country are very memorable (for example, their first interview for *Le Grand Journal* in 'La Boîte A Questions' was epic; the boys were just goofy and fun, just as we love them). Apart from being talented and handsome, the fact that some of them can actually speak French a little is definitely a plus for us, which makes them even more attractive.'

Some of the boys funny answers from the *Le Grand Journal* interview:
'Who is the French President?'
Niall: 'Jacques Chirac.'
Louis: 'Captain Jack Sparrow.'
'What underwear are you wearing tonight?'
Louis: 'I'm wearing Topman boxers.'
Niall: 'I'm wearing Calvin Klein.'
Liam: 'Ralph Lauren Polo!'

They were also asked to raise the temperature in less than 30 seconds. Louis pretended to boil a kettle, Niall and Zayn pretended to run, Liam jumped up and down, Harry did star jumps and then rubbed his nipples. When Louis' pretended the kettle had boiled, he imitated throwing it over the others, and they all screamed as if they had been burned. The boys love any excuse to mess around and have a laugh.

They had to impersonate one of their fans, so Zayn put on a squeaky voice and said, 'Louis, I love your bum!'

Their final challenge was to strip tease, so Harry started to take off his jacket and Zayn went to open his shirt until Niall pressed the button to end the interview.

SALOMÉ'S STORY

Salomé is 18 and from Troyes in north-central France. She became a 1D fan in January 2011. She met Harry, Niall, Liam, Zayn and Louis on Valentine's Day 2012 in Paris. She had heard on Twitter that they would be at the Virgin Megastore on the Champs-Elysées and knew she had to go see them. There were 700 girls there, all very excited. Salomé thought the boys looked gorgeous: Zayn was wearing a white T-shirt and a leather jacket, Niall and Liam were wearing white T-shirts as well, Louis was wearing a maroon sweater and Harry was wearing a white T-shirt with a grey blazer.

She says, 'The boys were amazing and adorable and,

when I met them, I was about to give them my CD to get it signed but a security guard told me they weren't allowed to sign anymore. Niall saw I was a bit disappointed so he did, like, an 'I'm sorry' face and then he smiled at me and took my hand. It was amazing. Then I saw Zayn, Liam and Louis, and got to shake their hands.

'Then Harry, aha ... Let's be clear, I love ALL the boys, but I have a huge crush on Harry. I was just speechless, I tried to explain to him how much he means to me, and he said, *"Je t'aime,"* which means "I love you" in French. I couldn't move or speak, I wasn't able to do anything and I know it's stupid, because I'm not the only one who loves them, but the fact they knew my existence for one minute makes me feel good.

EMMA'S STORY

Emma is 18 and from Paris. She has met the boys four times. Harry follows her on Twitter. The first time she met them was Valentine's Day 2012 at a signing. The second time was when they were recording a TV show called *Le Grand Journal*. Because it was the school holidays, lots of fans waited for them to arrive at the train station and it was very manic. The boys got mobbed by fans and Liam even lost a shoe. Emma had a ticket to be in the audience and so got to stand really close to them. As they sang 'What Makes You Beautiful', Zayn made eye contact with Emma and lots of girls got jealous; poor Emma ended up getting hit by the girls around her – not nice at all.

The third time Emma met the boys was on 11 November 2012 at a press conference. She says, 'As 1D only stay a day in Paris when they come to promote their albums, they decided to give a press conference. It was their first one. Only four fans were there and I was one of them. People from magazines asked them some stuff about their new album, their new life as famous people, etc. 1D acted as usual. Some of their answers were quite random; whenever they got asked questions about girls, they would look at each other and smile. Liam almost fell off the stage at one point when Louis split his water bottle.

'The fourth time I met them was at a special showcase. It was a private showcase, so fans could only get tickets if they had won a radio competition. I, however, was invited by the boys' management because I promote the boys in France. It was amazing to see them live because it was the first time since *The X Factor* tour that I had seen them perform. They were so confident! It impressed me how, in two years, they had gotten used to the stage and are now able to 'play' with their voices, which are now so much more

143

mature. They flirted a lot with fans during the performance. I took a poster with my Twitter name and Harry recognised it and waved. It's incredible how they remember the fans they have met before or that they have followed on Twitter. When they're allowed to take pictures with fans, they're so sweet and get as close as possible to them.'

MARINE'S STORY

Marine is 16 and from Montpellier, a town in the south of France. She met the boys on 2 November 2011 at Le Bourget Airport in Paris. It was 1.30am and the boys were pretty tired from their flight. She managed to speak to Liam, Harry and Zayn briefly, and Niall gave her a wave. When the boys were in their car, Marine and her friends tried to run alongside the vehicle but Paul from the 1D security team told them that it was dangerous to follow because they were going too fast, so Marine stopped.

She went home to sleep but then went to the hotel where she thought the boys were staying at 1pm in the hope of catching a glimpse of them coming back from their showcase. She managed to see Liam through the glass of their vehicle but decided that the best place to wait for them would be back at the airport, as they could be flying out that night.

FRANCE

'I bought a French flag with my friends Julie, Audrey, Alexane and Agathe,' Marine says. 'And we wrote our nicknames in French and English. When we saw the boys, Harry took the flag from us and said, *"Merci."* He also signed my yearbook and posed for photos with the others.

'I would say to anyone who wants to meets the boys that it is possible; you just need to make it happen. I had to wait for 12 hours but it was well worth it.'

If you want to follow Marine on Twitter, her Twitter name is @CatchStyles.

CHAPTER THIRTEEN

GERMANY

The boys were famous in Germany before 'What Makes You Beautiful' had been released in the country. Niall admitted to *Bravo WebTV* in October 2011, 'Well, obviously in Germany they didn't get to see us on *The X Factor* so all they know us from is, like, YouTube and Twitter, which is kind of mind blowing for us because obviously our UK fans know us from *The X Factor* and stuff. It's kinda strange how people find out about things. The power of the Internet is really strong.'

Louis added, 'It makes us amazingly proud; it's such a crazy thing. I don't think we feel famous here yet but the support we have here already is just incredible. It's just really flattering.'

GERMANY

Germany narrowly missed out on winning the Bring 1D To Me competition, which was won by Holland, Sweden and Italy, but the boys gave German fans a second chance because they had been so close to winning. A message on their website read, 'The boys really wanted to give you one last chance to win the final air miles so we've laid down a final challenge! We want 1,000 signatures on this Bring 1D To Me Twitter petition by midnight on Sunday, 11 September. If you get all the signatures, 1D will be coming to Germany too! Good luck and we hope that you can Bring 1D To you!'

German fans managed to get more than 1,000 signatures, so the boys made their trip on 4 October 2011. As well as doing a signing, they performed for fans and answered some questions too.

A month after their first trip, they performed at *The Dome*, a massive TV show and music event, which is held every three months.

DID YOU KNOW?

Harry's uncle and cousin live in Hamburg, Germany and, on his first visit to the country with Liam, Louis, Zayn and Niall, he couldn't remember if he had been before when he was younger or not but thought he probably had. The others had never been before.

After the boys had been to Germany a few times, they were asked by the German *X Factor* host on the red carpet of the Bambi Awards what makes German Directioners special. Louis replied, 'I suppose just their support; you know, we've been here three or four times and the support every time has just been absolutely incredible, so we can't really thank them enough for that.'

The first nationwide German 1D flash mob happened on 19 May 2012 in 17 German cities. It was choreographed by D!'s Dance Club! To see the video, search on YouTube for 'One Direction – Flash mob Germany'. Flash mobs happened in Berlin, Hamburg, Munich, Cologne, Hannover, Dortmund and Stuttgart, as well as in other cities. At the end of the video, you can see some funny outtakes of football fans that got in the way of the cameras.

The winners of the German Go1Den ticket were Isabelle and Nhu, whose video received the most votes. Their video was a 30-second 1D rap based on the 'Fresh Prince of Bel-Air'. Check it out on YouTube by searching for 'Muc3'.

EMMA'S STORY

Emma is 19 and from Ronse in Belgium. She met the boys on Saturday, 22 September at the MediaPark in

Above: Megan from the UK loved meeting Niall and Louis and managed to give them both a kiss on their cheeks!

Below: Megan couldn't stop smiling when she met Harry backstage.

One Direction may have fans all around the world now, but even in the X-Factor days there was no rest for the boys… Here, Harry returns home from the show to find his front garden taken over by adoring youngsters!

Magda from the UK couldn't resist giving Louis a piggyback!

Above: Niall was feeling tired in this photo with Liam and Magda.

Below: Harry looks so cute in his beanie hat and vest!

Above: Meeting One Direction in New York was a dream come true for Victoria from Austria.

Below: Chile Directioners join together to wish Liam a Happy 19th Birthday.

Above: A group of fans in Sydney, Australia, hold up an incredible collage of One Direction photos and memorabilia – in the shape of a London bus! ©*Rex Features*

Below: Home is where the heart is: Louis Tomlinson returns to his old school with Liam Payne. Louis gets a hug from an old teacher as Liam signs autographs.

© *Rex Features*

Harry and the other boys are happy to sign whatever their fans want them to, at any time.

© Rex Features

A key memento for any Directioner is a photo with the boys. Names clockwise from top left: The Chile Directioners, the Greek Directioners, Nicole, Shannice, Tiffani, Maria, Magda and finally, the boys with Josca's beautiful artwork.

Cologne, Germany's fourth-biggest city. She made lots of friends while she was waiting to see Harry, Zayn, Louis, Niall and Liam. 'It only took a few minutes of chatting to build up a friendship,' she reveals. 'We all loved One Direction so much. We had slept on the cold hard ground of the MediaPark together and shared blankets, food and our stories. The rest of the world could say whatever they wanted; we had each other. And we all had the same goal: meeting our boys.'

After waiting 24 hours, Emma and her friends were only moments away from meeting the boys when one of her new friends, Natalie, got really nervous and asked Emma if she would stay with her. Emma promised she would and they stood in line and headed for the stage where the boys were all sitting.

Emma takes up the story: 'I heard Natalie say, "They're real, this is real, they're actually here!" as soon as she spotted them. I turned to look at her and saw tears of happiness pouring down her face, as I felt hot tears running down mine as well. It had been a battle, we'd had to stay so long in the cold and there'd been fights with the girls who tried to get in front of us. We'd had no sleep, no food, we'd been standing up for nine hours straight. I knew that she understood me completely and that was all I needed; we turned back to the stage where the boys were posing for the cameras.

'The security guard bellowed that we were on and that we had to move. I looked back at Natalie one last time and we nodded. I climbed the few stairs that separated me from the stage. Up there another security guard waited and looked me up and down, head to toe. I had a paper in my hand, a little letter that my friend had asked me to give to Liam, and five little camera-shaped water guns, which I had bought for the boys. He looked at the paper and took it from me. "But it's for Liam," I muttered, but he didn't care. I quickly hid my water guns and managed to sneak them past him.'

Emma almost tripped over her feet when she took the last step separating her from Zayn, who sat first at the table. She swallowed the lump in her throat and managed to hold back the tears. 'I put the cover of my DVD on the table so the boys could sign it,' she remembers. 'Zayn looked up at me and said hi. I swallowed again and put one of the cameras on the table. "I got you something," I managed to say. He looked at the camera, then back at me. "What is it?" he asked (which made my knees go weak). "Push it," I told him. I managed to stop him just in time from squirting the water in his own face. "Oh, is it water?" he asked, realising what it was. I nodded and he smiled. "Thank you!" he said before he aimed the gun between me and Natalie. I smiled.

GERMANY

Never had I expected him to be so sweet and he was actually happy with a stupid gift, him being a millionaire and all.

'Next was Harry, then Louis, then Liam and, last but not least at all, Niall. They were all really sweet and caring and they seemed genuinely happy. When it was over, I just froze and the security guard pushed me towards the exit of the stage. Everything after that is one big blur. I remember looking back and finding Natalie. We broke down in sobs and had to sit down on the ground to catch our breath. My heart was still racing and images passed before my eyes. I had never ever in my life felt this way.'

If you want to follow Emma on, her Twitter name is @stylesandpotter.

CHAPTER FOURTEEN

GREECE

On 21 July 2012, more than 120 Greek Directioners descended on Syntagma Square in Athens for a flash mob. They danced for over six minutes and did an amazing job. The five girls at the front wore red vests with KEEP CALM AND BRING ONE DIRECTION TO GREECE on the front and they each had a boy's name on their backs. The girls had spent hours making huge banners asking the boys to visit Greece.

The organisers posted a video on YouTube with the message, 'We want to thank all the Greek Directioners who came and did this with us, you were all amazing! A HUGE thank you to Athens Deejay radio for helping us to make one of our dreams come true and for all the support. Also, we wanna thank the girls from the other flash mobs who inspired us to do this, Flash mob L.A., Flash mob Finland, Flash mob Sydney etc.

'Thanks to Dimitra who recorded the whole flash mob and the girls who took us pictures :)

'I personally wanna thank the other four girls who made the choreography, I love you guys, you are my flawless angels :):)'

To see the video, search 'One Direction Flash mob Greece'.

Superfan Ourania, who is 14, sums up why she thinks One Direction have so many fans in Greece: 'They make us laugh so much with the silly things they do. They not only have amazing voices, but they are just normal guys who like the same things we do.'

Greek Directioner Joanna, who is 19, can't put her finger on one thing that makes them so popular. 'The reasons why we love them are countless,' she says. 'They are so talented and beautiful; they enjoy their lives and live life to the fullest. All of them are perfect in their own way. Greece loves One Direction and we pray that they will come to visit us soon.'

Eighteen-year-old Artemi says, 'My life has dramatically changed because of these five beautiful, adorable, funny and very talented boys. Whatever happens, I will always support them with all my heart, even if I never ever have the opportunity to see them from close.'

DIMITRA'S STORY

Dimitra is 15 and from Thessaloniki. She says, 'To be a Directioner here in Greece is a little bit weird: we don't get to hear things about the music world as fast as other countries. I found out about the boys one year after they'd been on *The X Factor*. I found a video of them on YouTube by mistake. From that moment, I started searching more and more, finding out who they were, their lives and how they came to be where they are today. So, little by little, I became one of their fans, joining millions of other girls from all around the world. I also got to meet some other Greek Directioners from different areas! I haven't had the pleasure of seeing them perform live yet but hope to one day, I will never stop supporting them.'

VASILIA'S STORY

Vasilia is 15 and from Athens. If she had to choose a favourite member of the band and a favourite song, she would have to say Liam and the song 'More Than This'. She tries to ignore the haters who say nasty things about the boys and their fans, she says, because 'nothing is gonna stop me from supporting these boys, who have changed my whole life. Every day I tweet them in the hope that they will notice me, every single day I want them to be happy, I want the best for them. I can't explain how much they mean to me. Because of them I have made so many true friends, that I never had before, my 1D family.'

The boys love receiving tweets from fans and, even though they can't reply to every tweet individually, they appreciate each one. One day Vasilia may receive a tweet back or even a follow from one of the boys – and that would mean the world to her.

MARIA AND NATALIE'S STORY

Maria and Natalie are two best friends from Thessaloniki. They are 18 years old. Natalie was the first to find out about the boys and she introduced their music to Maria.

Natalie says, 'To be honest, being a Directioner in our country is not the easiest thing to do. People criticise fans for supporting the boys; they say things like, "Why do you care so much about them, do you really think you'll marry them? You know nothing about their lives and they know nothing about your lives." Or, they'll say things like, "It's just another boy band; they will fade away in a few years."'

Maria adds, 'Some people think we only care about their looks. But they're so wrong. Like, seriously, why did we buy their albums then? To listen to their faces?

No. We like them for who they are. We like their amazing voices. They inspire us to be better people. And that's why we thank them for entering our lives.

'Luckily, the Greek Directioner family is strong and united. We organise meet-ups to get to know each other. There, we sing One Direction Songs, talk about our lives and interests; generally, we bond with each other. We also do flash mobs, to make the boys notice us. We have loads of fun there. That's a positive aspect of our lives as Directioners in Greece. All in all, although we experience some difficulties, we have good times and that's all that matters.'

RITSA'S STORY

Ritsa is 18 and lives on the island of Crete. She became a Directioner on her birthday after her friend dedicated one of their songs to her. She joined the Greek team on 25 November and made so many friends. She can't choose a favourite 1D song – she loves 'Moments', 'Little Things' and 'More Than This' equally. She says, 'At our meet-ups we have awesome experiences! All Directioners are crazy! We make many things together, sing, dance. I didn't go to the first flash mob because I wasn't a fan then, but I'll be definitely taking part in the second one we do. I can't wait.'

CHAPTER FIFTEEN

IRELAND

Niall might live in London now when he's not touring the world with 1D, but Ireland will always be his home. He was so happy when *Up All Night* was released in Ireland as it meant his family could walk into any record shop and pick up an album of his music. It was something he had wanted for such a long time.

> **DID YOU KNOW?**
> Niall auditioned for *The X Factor* at Croke Park Stadium in Dublin.

It meant the world to him when *Up All Night* charted at number one in Ireland – it only made number two in the UK. At the time, Niall had no idea that it would end up being released worldwide and would be number one in America, Australia, Canada, Croatia, Italy, Mexico, New Zealand, Sweden and many more countries.

The first single One Direction released was 'What Makes You Beautiful' and it was number one in Ireland, the UK, US and Mexico, number two in New Zealand, number three in Japan, number seven in Australia and Canada, and did well in other countries too. Liam said at the time that the boys felt humbled to have 'What Makes You Beautiful' do so well, telling BBC Radio 1, 'We have an incredible team of people around us who have helped us achieve this. Above all, we would like to thank our fans. We owe all our success to them.'

The Up All Night Tour might have been to the UK, America, Canada, Mexico, Australia and New Zealand, but Niall's favourite performance has to be their show in Dublin. He tweeted in the lead-up to the concert, 'IRELAND we are coming ... been waiting for this day all my life!' and 'I cannot wait! Lets pull the roof off the O2 tomorrow night!'

On the morning of the show, he tweeted, 'Today is a very special day for me! I literally cannot wait! #1DinDublin'.

After the show, he tweeted, 'Ireland! Absolutely

incredible is an understatement! Thank you for a lovely welcome home! Had goosebumps all night and a tear in my eye!'

He then added, '#Irishandproud small nation but we can sure make a hell of a lot of noise! Love you all! Dream come true.'

One Direction have millions of fans around the world from virtually every country, but Niall would like to see more boys liking their music. He told Tumblr's *Storyboard* blog, 'We want to see more boy fans, as seeing them in the crowd is cool … it's 90 per cent girls, but we want to expand our fan base. We want all people to like us.'

Liam explained that the whole group are very grateful to every fan that goes out, buys tickets to their concerts, and supports them. 'It's very flattering obviously as we can see how much they care for us,' he said. 'We just hope they're crying tears of joy! None of us could obviously ever have imagined this just two years ago. I don't think anyone could have seen this coming to be honest.'

DID YOU KNOW?

Niall struggles to cope when he gets surrounded by hundreds of fans. His dad Bobby told the

Mirror, 'There are hordes of young girls around him, and not much room to breathe anywhere. He says it can be frightening. Coming out of airports and girls crowding around their cars, he's started to get really claustrophobic.'

Despite Niall coming from Ireland, Irish Directioners haven't had many opportunities to meet the band. In 2011, Niall only spent 30 days in his home country. Superfan Grainne explains, 'People seem to think just because Niall is from here that we get a lot of meet-and-greets, signings, concerts, visits, but this isn't the case. We've had one signing and a few fans were selected to meet the boys and get their album signed. The boys only did one concert for the Up All Night Tour and I sadly didn't get tickets. I am proud to call myself a Directioner but it is very hard to always be so ecstatic that the boys are getting big all around the world because it means small countries like Ireland will get less visits than they already have, which is very little.'

REBECCA'S STORY

Rebecca is 17 and from Dublin. She has met the boys lots of times. The first time was on 19 August 2011 when they were in Dublin promoting 'What Makes You Beautiful' at different radio stations. She followed them around as they went to Spin 1038, FM104, 98FM and Q102, and, finally, after waiting 15 hours to speak to them, she managed to. They chatted about the single and exchanged pleasantries.

'Three days later they came back to Dublin for the wedding of their tour manager Paul,' Rebecca reveals. 'Nobody knew of this except me and a few friends, so we went to the airport to meet them. We got to spend a good while with them, taking pictures, talking and joking. This was 22 August and it was probably the best day of my life.

'Thirdly, after camping for two whole days, we got wristbands to meet them on 19 November 2011 in Clare Hall Shopping Centre. They had signings for their album *Up All Night*. It was well worth the wait and queuing because they're genuinely the nicest boys ever. I also gave Harry a Christmas stocking with the words 'Caroline Flack' on the front as a joke, back when the rumours of them first started. Everyone was laughing about it, even Harry, and that night he tweeted about the day at the signing, also saying 'PS thanks for my stocking.xx'. That honestly made my life and Harry Styles is probably the nicest person you will ever come across in your life.

'On 26 November 2011, they were back in Dublin

for an interview on *The Late Late Show*. I was in Dublin City with my school year that day because we were going to the cinema, and we saw the boys on their bus in Temple Bar. I was unbelievably shocked but it was definitely a great surprise.'

DID YOU KNOW?

While the boys were at Paul's wedding, they took part in two Marryoke videos – check out the videos on YouTube; they are fantastic and really give you an insight into what it was like at the wedding. To see the videos, just go to YouTube and type in 'Marryoke Paul and Clodagh'.

JENN'S STORY

Jenn is 15 and from Limerick. She met Harry, Niall, Liam, Louis and Zayn on 19 November 2011 in Maynooth, Co. Kildare at a book and album signing. She gave Liam a gift bag filled with the band's favourite sweets, she gave Zayn a pair of black earrings, and for her favourite member Niall she had a leprechaun badge. She also told Niall he was gorgeous and this made him blush!

IRELAND

CIARA'S STORY

Ciara is 15 and from Dublin. She is an Irish Directioner and is part of the 1D Irish Street Team: their Twitter account is @1DIrishSignings. Ciara and her friends Sally, Sorcha and Caoimhe, are campaigning for a signing over in Ireland. She has met the boys twice: the first time was outside the RTÉ Studios when the boys were on *The Late Late Show*, and the second was outside their hotel in Dublin before a concert. She says, 'Sometimes the boys aren't allowed to pose for fans, which is really disappointing. My advice for fans is to keep trying. If you are from Ireland, please follow us on Twitter and join our campaign.'

CHAPTER SIXTEEN

MEXICO

Mexico was the only country in North America that the boys visited aside from the USA and Canada with their Up All Night Tour. They planned two concerts during the World Tour 2013 – performing at Foro Sol in Mexico City on 8 and 9 June. It was to be just over a year since they had last performed there, as their dates for the Up All Night Tour had been 5 and 6 June 2012.

Shortly before the boys visited Mexico for the first time, Niall tweeted fans to say, 'Our first time in south america! Mexico here we come! Cannot wait, ive heard audiences down there are crazy! #1DinMexico #vivamexico'.

In a tweet Niall wrote on 18 June 2012, he said,

MEXICO

'Been to so many countries now! Sweden,germany, france,italy,holland,australia,newzealand,mexico, US,canada, loving this journey,its been sick'. Niall had always wanted to travel to thank fans in each country for supporting them and making their dreams come true.

For Mexico's Bring Me to 1D event, fans had to complete a series of challenges. The winner was Daniela; the10 runners-up each won two tickets to the sold out World Tour.

The boys love visiting Mexico, with Zayn admitting during an interview with *HOY*, 'We were just kinda blown away by the response that we get from our fans, and yet again you know, our fans in Mexico kind of delivered and it's been amazing, it's been really cool. The only word I could really use to describe Mexican fans is passionate.'

Louis added 'loud', as he thinks that sums up Mexican fans. All the boys are grateful for the support from Mexican fans, especially because a lot of fans don't speak English.

Mexican fans joined together to do a flash mob in April 2012. If you want to see it, go to YouTube and search for 'One Direction Chihuahua, Mexico Flash Mob.' They are currently planning their choreography for their next one, so Mexican fans who want to be involved should join the One

Direction Chihuahua page on Facebook. Alternatively you could join the main One Direction Mexico page, which has over 70,000 fans.

CHAPTER SEVENTEEN

NETHERLANDS

In October 2011, the boys made their first trip to the Netherlands as part of the Bring 1D to Me competition. They did a signing, answered some questions and did an acoustic version of 'What Makes You Beautiful', with Niall playing his guitar.

In November 2011, the boys launched a special Sinterklaas (Santa Claus) competition just for Dutch fans. Via video, the boys explained what fans had to do.

Liam said, 'Hi, Holland, we've heard that on 5 December you guys celebrate Sinterklaas. We also heard that you leave your shoe outside the door or in front of your chimney and, when you're sleeping, he brings you presents.'

Harry continued, 'So here's the deal. We want you guys to upload a picture of your shoe with a nice little gift to us in it and in return we're gonna give a small gift to you. Enjoy!'

To see what sort of things Dutch fans get up to, check out the 1dHolland channel on YouTube. There is a great video called 'Bring 1D To Holland – My experience 04/05.10.201', which is well worth checking out as it shows what happened during their one-day visit from a fan's perspective. You'll see Niall high-fiving the crowd and Liam wearing the Dutch flag on his back. You'll also see them at the fan event itself, performing 'What Makes You Beautiful'.

During an interview with the RTL TV station, the boys were asked about dating someone in front of a worldwide audience and Zayn replied, 'If people are interested in your relationship, let them be, but I don't think you should ever publically explain your relationship to people – that's between you and your girlfriend.'

In the same interview, Louis said, 'All our mothers have all our money and we still get pocket money every week. That's the truth.' Louis wasn't being serious though and, when the interviewer said he didn't believe him, Louis jokingly said, 'How dare you!' His comeback when the journalist mentioned the expensive houses they had bought was that 'property's cheap at the moment'.

The boys didn't perform their Up All Night Tour in the Netherlands, but for the World Tour they had one show in Amsterdam's Ziggo Zone on 3 May.

The Bring Me to 1D competition was run by Q-Music radio station, who invited the Netherland's biggest One Direction fans to their studio to take a 1D exam. The exam was really tough and the girls with the two highest scores made it through to the final round. They were asked even harder questions and, after a tense wait, Jessica was announced as the winner who would be going to New York.

ROO'S STORY

Roo is 15 and from Eindhoven. Her favourite member of One Direction is Harry Styles and, if she had to choose a favourite song, she would have to pick 'She's Not Afraid'. She has taken part in the 1D flash mobs in her country and goes to 1D camp too. Roo explains, 'We have a 1Dcamp four times a year. Directioners come along to a place for three days, and they sleep in a house and do some 1D-related things. We perform like the boys for each other and play some games to try and win 1D prizes.'

One of the flash mobs took place in Utrecht on 26 February 2012. It was organised by @onednews, with

Directioners Laura and Kim organising the choreography and Marlous and Iris filming it. Forty Dutch Directioners took part.

EMMA'S STORY

Emma is 15 and from Emmen in the northeast of the Netherlands. She explains how she became a Directioner: 'I live in the Netherlands, so I couldn't watch *The X Factor* on my TV and I didn't follow the shows. However, I was searching on the Internet and a video of the boys showed up. I watched the video and liked it, so I listened to them for the whole week. A month later, my best friend told me she liked a boyband and I searched for them on YouTube. Turned out it was the same band! I searched for more videos and more information about each boy and became a real fan.'

When Emma found out that the boys were coming to her country on 5 October 2011, she was thrilled. In the weeks leading up to their visit, fans had to play a series of games organised by their promoters in the Netherlands and the more games they played, the bigger the chance they would have to get a code. If you had one of the codes, you could meet the boys.

'My friend and I won a code, so we could meet the boys,' Emma says. 'There were only 500 codes, so we were very lucky! I travelled to the other side of Holland. Before we went in the Hotel Arena in Amsterdam, we got a badge and a blank signature card. The presenter asked the boys a few questions and then they sang "What Makes You Beautiful". It was great! Their voices were even better in real life and everyone was so happy and kind to each other! After an hour and a half, we could have a little talk with them and let them sign our card. My friend and I made little bags with presents for the boys and we gave it to them. They were so nice to me and they looked even better with only a few metres between us! But I was nervous – too nervous. I didn't say very much, but the boys tried to let me feel at ease – very sweet. Louis even called me "love"! It was the best day of my life and I'm so glad that I had the chance to meet them!'

JOSCA'S STORY

Josca is 17 and from Meppel, also in the northeast of the Netherlands. And she also met the boys at the Bring 1D To Me Event on 5 October 2011. She took with her five drawings to give to the boys and a collage made up of scanned images of the five drawings so that the boys could sign that and she could bring it home as a memento. 'With a tube filled with the five drawings and the collage in my left hand, and a camera in the other hand, my friend and I joined the crowd of teenage girls at the hotel,' she says. 'It was, like, the loudest crowd I've ever heard; I didn't know girls could produce such a loud noise! I covered my ears with the tube and my arm when the boys came on the stage to answer some questions. It was deafening. After the question-and-answer (I couldn't hear anything of what One Direction had said because of the noise), my friend and I were waiting in line for the signing. I was really nervous.'

At the signing table, Josca was scared she wouldn't be able to give her drawings to the boys because security were strict and were only letting everyone have one thing signed. 'At first I put the collage with all the drawings in front of Liam on the table,' Josca continues. 'I remember I didn't even say hi because I was nervous – how rude! Anyway, Liam immediately looked at it and I heard him saying, "Wait, are those drawings?" Niall, who was sitting next to him, screamed, "What the hell!" I laughed and showed them the original drawings I was holding in my hands. Niall mumbled something as I gave Liam and him the drawings I'd made of them. He looked at me with his blue eyes wide open and I can't even describe how I felt at that moment. It was an amazing feeling. He assured me several times he was going to frame his drawing. Liam had put his drawing on a chair behind him. Meanwhile, I'd laid the other drawings on the table in front of the lads because I was scared it would be over too soon, as the security were pushing the girls in line. Zayn didn't do anything but bite his lip and hold the drawing in front of him with his arms oustretched as he looked at it proudly. Louis looked at me with a pretty weird look on his face while Harry was talking to me.

'I said something like, "I am so happy right now!" When I was about to arrive at Harry, he looked at me with sparkles in his green eyes and I got carried away a little, I have to admit. He asked me, "Did you draw this?" holding my drawing in his hands. I said yes and he answered, "You're so talented!" I actually couldn't hear what he said the first time because of screaming girls behind us in front of the stage, so I put my face a bit closer to his and he said it again, "You're so talented!" I then answered him again, "Thank you so much! I think I spent around 10 hours on this one and the others even more!" Harry was surprised and said, "Thank you, thank you!" The last thing I said to him when I had to leave the stage again was a little, "You're welcome", and then it was over.

'My friend and I went outside and we couldn't stop talking about it. My mum went shopping in Amsterdam and, after we got out of the hotel, I called her, being all happy and jumpy. I just couldn't believe that some people I'd admired for such a long time, admired me for a moment, for what I'd done. When my mum arrived at the hotel she hugged me tightly and told me she was so happy for me; she actually cried tears of happiness.'

To see the boys with Josca's drawings, check out the picture section in this book.

Josca concludes, 'The next day I was looking through the photos my friend had taken and wondered what the guys would be doing with the drawings. I got really scared their management might have taken them away, but then the pictures appeared on the Internet. The boys were each holding up the drawings I had done of them – it was unbelievable and I burst into tears. My mum wondered what was going on!'

Josca would love to meet the boys again one day and her ultimate dream is to get to sing with them one day.

CHAPTER EIGHTEEN

NEW ZEALAND

The boys loved their mini-tour of New Zealand in 2012; they performed in Auckland's Trusts Stadium and Wellington's St James Theatre. In an interview with The Edge radio station about their first trip to New Zealand, Liam was asked what the difference would be between the current show they were putting on in Auckland compared to their up-and-coming World Tour show in 2013. He said, 'So this weekend we're doing our tour that we've been doing for a while now, called Up All Night, and then next year we're doing a different tour with a new album, maybe some new things in the show as well, and maybe just in general a bigger show because we're gonna be playing bigger arenas and stuff.

There's more seats to fill so we just want to put on the best show possible really.'

During their visit Harry went out with the American model in the 'Gotta Be You' video, Emma Ostilly, one night. The paparazzi managed to photograph them kissing outside the place Emma was staying in the early hours of the morning after Harry had dropped her off. Harry was questioned about their date the next day but he told reporters that he'd been in bed by 11pm and so they must have been misinformed. He also wouldn't talk about Emma and just wanted to talk about their music and their shows in New Zealand. Harry might have maintained a dignified silence but Emma still received abuse from some fans on Twitter. In fact, she received so many horrible messages that she temporarily shut down her Twitter account.

When Liam was asked what he made of New Zealand in the short time they'd been there by TV3's *3 News*, he said, 'Well, I've heard that it's the place where they invented the bungee jump, so I wanna try out where they invented the bungee jump.'

Zayn wasn't up for it though because he has a fear of heights. In the end it was Liam and Louis who did the jump at the legendary Sky Tower, which is the tallest manmade structure in New Zealand.

To win the Kiwi Go1Den ticket, fans had to listen to ZM radio every day so they could find the 1D phone booth and call a special number. Fans who managed this went into a draw and the name picked out was Olivia from Christchurch.

For the World Tour 2013, the boys planned three dates in New Zealand, performing at the CBS Canterbury Arena on 10 October and Auckland's Vector Arena on 12 and 13 October.

GINA'S STORY

Gina is 18 and from Whangarei in the North Island. She became a fan of the band right from the beginning, watching all the episodes of *The X Factor* online. She really wished she could have seen them live on TV but the episodes weren't shown there. She hasn't had a tweet from the boys but her friend Ellen received a tweet from Liam in 2010 telling her he was surprised to hear that they had fans in New Zealand.

'It's quite hard being a fan from New Zealand,' Gina says, 'because you read all the tweets about how the boys are in the UK or the USA, and they don't seem to come to New Zealand very often. It's really hard to get noticed by them on Twitter because Liam's the only one who actually re-tweets people and does follow sprees and such.

'I have met some amazing people over Twitter, who are also fans, and I don't know if the boys know how much people unite over them, but we do. We make friends online who are sometimes nicer than the people we know in real life, and I think that's an important part of being in a fandom. We're all there for each other, even for things that are completely unrelated to One Direction. We're like a family that's worldwide. I'm in this fandom for the boys, but also for the friends I've made along the way. I've been there since the start. Every video diary. Every episode. Every tear. Every heartbreak. And I'll always be there. They're a part of my life now.'

JOSIE'S STORY

Josie is 47 and she lives in Hawera in the North Island with her daughters Brenna, 15, and Lana, 19, who are huge One Direction fans. Their favourite member is Harry. When Josie and her girls found out that the boys would be performing Up All Night concerts in New Zealand, they knew they had to be there. They managed to get tickets to the first concert and Josie drove them all the way to Auckland. Josie says, 'We took Brenna's friend Miraya (15) with us and it took us seven hours to get there. We put a sign saying we were going to see One Direction in the back window of our car and had some interesting interactions with other drivers on the way; it was hilarious!

'When we first arrived, I was able to park the car really close to the stadium. We got out and started getting organised ... next thing, the boys' black vehicle entered the car park and drove right by us to the entrance. There was no one else around, we were within a metre of the boys and could see them inside the vehicle! The girls ran after it and we got photos of the boys going in. It was a very exciting start!

'One Direction had two concerts in one day at the same venue and we went to the first one, at 2pm. It was absolutely fantastic! Even though we were in the very back row we still felt very lucky to even be there when so many fans had missed out. During the concert Brenna and Miraya's good friends Rebecca and Brigid, both 15, had their tweet read out by the boys on stage – we couldn't believe it! (The tweet was 'Chocolate or rainbow paddlepops?' Zayn picked chocolate and Harry said, 'I've never tried rainbow paddlepops but I'm going to vote for them anyway'.)

'After the concert, we knew the boys were still in the stadium so we waited around hoping to get a glimpse of them ... Zayn came out and Brenna and Miraya called out, "Zayn!" He turned to them and gave them a big wave; they were absolutely elated! We knew the evening concert was sold out so we were preparing to go home.'

However, the girls were really lucky as just then an official came out and told them that there were actually some tickets still available for the evening concert. They went to the ticket stand and couldn't believe their luck – they could get four seats in a row, in the 11th row, centre stage!

Josie continues the story: 'So thank goodness for my Visa card. I snapped up those tickets immediately and we all went to the evening concert as well. It was SO amazing, definitely one of the best days ever! Being so close to the stage in the second concert was incredible – we were close enough to see the boys very clearly and get covered in the white 'snow' that came out, and we nearly caught a ball! We felt very lucky to think we went from the very back of the stadium in the first concert to the 11th row in the second concert all in one day. WAHOO!!!

'When we got home, concert dates for 2013 were announced and we straight away got tickets for the October 2013 concert to be held once again in Auckland, only this time we are going one step better ...we have tickets for the Soundcheck Party, centre stage in row three!'

If you want to follow Josie on Twitter, her Twitter name is @NewZealand1D.

CHAPTER NINETEEN

NORWAY

Sometimes the boys will do interviews in London for TV shows in other countries. This was the case when the presenters from Norway's talk show *Senkveld* came over and interviewed the boys. Harry told them about the first time they'd seen themselves in the UK newspapers. 'I remember there was one morning when we'd heard that we were in the paper and it was the first time that we'd been in the paper,' he said. 'All of us went to the shop and got this paper and we were, like, gathered around this paper, reading it, and we were, like, "Our picture's in the paper, it's got out!"'

DID YOU KNOW?

The picture in the newspaper was actually taken by Louis' mum of them on some stairs.

Norwegian fans were so excited when they found out that Harry, Niall, Liam, Louis and Zayn would be going to Norway as part of their World Tour in 2013 and would be playing at the Telenor Arena in Baerum on 7 May, as they hadn't managed to visit with their Up All Night Tour.

VICTORIA'S STORY

Victoria is 16 and from Oslo. Her biggest wish was to meet One Direction but she had no idea how she would meet them until she found out about the Bring Me To 1D fan event. On their website, the boys wrote, 'All across the world, Go1Den Tickets are being released. Winners will get to take a friend and a guardian to see the boys perform at their Madison Square Garden gig in New York City on 3 December PLUS get a VIP invitation to attend a very special day on 4 December with the boys!'

Victoria wanted to enter, but she knew it wouldn't be easy: so many fans in her country would want to go. The challenge for Norwegians was to get as many people as possible to say 'I love One Direction' and to film a video of it. She had to think of something really creative and knew the perfect person to help her – her best friend Jina. Their video is incredible; check it out by visiting vimeo.com/52333842. Victoria and Jina got hundreds of people to say it – even a water aerobics class in a swimming pool!

Once One Direction had picked the girls as their winners, the Norwegian comedian Nils Aadne was given the task of telling them. Victoria had been sent upstairs to tidy her room and was so shocked when Nils came up the stairs. They went to tell Jina together, but she spotted them before they got to her front door, and ran outside in the freezing cold. She didn't even have shoes on as she started crying and hugging Victoria in the snow. They were going to be flying over 3,000 miles to meet One Direction!

Victoria reveals what happened a few weeks later: 'We met the boys in New York, 4 December 2012. It was literally the best day ever! Jina and I got two minutes alone with the boys, which probably sounds like nothing, but for Directioners it's everything. To even be in the same room and lay our eyes on them is incredible. When I walked towards them, I was so excited, but I didn't cry, I didn't pass out. I just said, "Vas Happenin." It was a bit awkward, but oh well.

It was really weird seeing them in real life because they looked just like they do in pictures and I felt like I knew them. I was really starstruck, but at least I was able to talk!'

Victoria thought the lads were really laid back but also that they seemed quite tired. 'They'd had a concert at Madison Square Garden the night before, so I don't blame them,' she says. 'I asked them how they were, told them that I loved their gig and explained to them that Harry jumped right on me at the concert. I even managed to "rawr" at him, so the boys had a proper laugh. Harry seemed quite shocked but he rawred back at me. I am now known on Twitter and YouTube as the Rawr Girl, haha! They signed my *Dare To Dream* book, and it's so surreal to look at that book thinking that they've touched it. When it was time for pictures, I asked them if they could kiss my cheeks, and they just smiled and said yes. Harry and Liam kissed my cheeks and I held my Norwegian flag in my hands. My friend was sat beside me and she got a kiss from Zayn. We said our goodbyes and Harry said, "We'll see you downstairs." We walked out of the room and into an elevator and I suddenly burst out in tears. It was so many emotions at once, I just had to lie down. A security guard asked my dad if I was all right, so maybe that explains it. I was shaking like never before and everything felt so unreal. It was just like a dream! After the meeting, the boys sang three songs and answered some questions. I was really enjoying every second of it!'

DID YOU KNOW?

As well as meeting the boys in New York, Victoria flew to see them perform in Liverpool, England on 17 March 2013.

CHAPTER TWENTY

RUSSIA

The winner of Russia's Go1Den ticket was 14-year-old Katie from Ekaterinburg. She made a great video using plasticine figurines of the boys – check it out on YouTube by searching for 'One Direction Everything About You Plasticine Video'. What she managed to achieve is truly remarkable. The storyline is really funny – the boys get chased around by a Russian fan and paint a big 1D sign. When Katie went to meet the boys in New York, she wore a T-shirt with her 1D plasticine figurines on the front. She also gave them each their own T-shirt with their figurine on the front and all the boys were really impressed.

RUSSIA

JULIA'S STORY

Julia is 16 and from Kurgan in Russia. She has been a fan of 1D ever since she heard 'What Makes You Beautiful' for the first time. 'I fell in love,' she admits. 'Fell in love with their voices. Every day I learned about them. They teach fans that it is OK to just be yourself and have fun.

'I found many people who like them and we have many common interests. To be a Russian Directioner is very nice. There are already about 33,000 Directioners in Russia. We also love our neighbours: Ukraine, Belarus and Kazakhstan fans. Altogether we have about 55,000 fans. They're all great. And we are one family. Occasionally we have conflicts and disagreements, but that happens in almost every family. And we all love each other.

'We meet up and make dances together to their music. One day we painted on the pavement of the largest park in the city. We drew lots of pictures of the boys. It was so funny!'

CHAPTER TWENTY-ONE

SINGAPORE

To win Singapore's Go1Den ticket, fans had to pre-order *Take Me Home* and sign up for a special account. Eight hundred fans qualified for a series of challenges at Bugis+ shopping mall on Friday, 9 November 2012. From the 800 only 50 names were called at random to take part in the first round. The 50 fans had to answer a question about 1D; if they got it wrong, they were disqualified and another fan was randomly picked to take their place.

After 50 fans had got the question right, they were split into five groups and each fan was given a pack of letters that spelt out the name of a member of One Direction. The four fastest at putting together the name in every group made it through to the next round.

The third round saw the last 20 fans given a jar of baby carrots and they had to guess how many carrots were in the jar. The five fans that got the closest made it through to the fourth round. For the final round, the fans had to choose between five bowls of Chinese bean curd dessert ('tau huay'). Nadia picked the bowl which had the only golden chocolate coin hidden inside, which meant that she had won the Go1Den ticket and would be going to New York!

KAIYING'S STORY

Kaiying is 17 and from Singapore. Her Twitter name is @1Domg and she has been a Directioner since 2011. She explains, 'The boys have played a big part in my life and that's the reason why I dedicated so much of time to organise the #1DSingaporeFlashmob, as we call it.

'The 1D flash mob idea started on the Singapore Directioners Facebook page, which I created with my friends so that the Singaporean Directioners could "fangirl" together and keep in touch. I contacted Sony Music and also HOT FM 91.3 (radio DJ Boy Thunder, @Boythunder913), and we started planning. Even though nothing was confirmed yet, my friends and I created the track and the dance moves so we would be prepared. We took about two days to confirm everything and filmed tutorials, which we uploaded on the Facebook page so that fans could learn the moves.

'We went through meetings with Sony Music and 91.3 and we managed to get Nando's Singapore to support us. It was quite hard to coordinate everything but, finally, we confirmed the flash mob and chose to do it at three locations: Raffles City (a business district), Bugis Plaza (a mall) and Orchard Road (one of the busiest roads in Singapore). The flash mob was on 14 March 2012 (coincidentally, my birthday, haha!) :-). About 300 people took part, though the number fluctuated at the different locations. Nando's Singapore even got their mascot (the chicken) to come down to every location to dance with us!

'Our local newspaper, the *New Paper*, came down and interviewed me and some others regarding the flash mob and we were a two-page feature in the paper a few days later. When Boy Thunder (the radio DJ) went to Australia to interview 1D, they mentioned how they had watched the flash mob and said that they were impressed. I was so proud of what we had done when I heard this.'

If you want to see the flash mob, just search for 'Official 1D Singapore Flashmob' on YouTube. Kaiying is the girl in the white shirt and shorts in the front row. The video has been viewed over 140,000 times!

SINGAPORE

Kaiying has never met One Direction but she did win a radio competition to speak to Liam on the phone and ask him a few questions. She asked him to marry her and he agreed. She says, 'I think Singaporean Directioners are extremely dedicated, especially those that have stayed by the boys for such a long time. It's really difficult for Directioners like us to stay so dedicated, since we have never met and they don't even have plans to have a World Tour over here till 2014. But still, we love the boys just as much as any other fan from any other country and we are proud to say that we are very, very dedicated.'

CHAPTER TWENTY-TWO

SPAIN

Spain will always be a special place for the boys because it was the first place they travelled to as a group. They had to go to Simon's rented villa in Marbella, Spain for the 'judges house' round of *The X Factor*. It was there that they sang together for the first time and it was there that they found out that Simon had chosen them for *The X Factor* live shows.

Niall, in particular, loves to go on holiday with his family and friends to Marbella. During one holiday, the paparazzi photographed him at The Ocean Club having fun in the pool. The press tried to link him to some girls who were there but he was only being friendly and chatting to them.

DID YOU KNOW?

Niall was actually on holiday in Spain when he got the phone call from *The X Factor* to say that he had been chosen to audition in front of Simon Cowell, Cheryl Cole, Louis Walsh and Katy Perry. Thankfully, his audition wasn't until he got home.

Spanish fans were so excited when they found out that the boys would be performing in Barcelona on 22 May and in Madrid on 24 and 25 May on their World Tour 2013. They rushed out to get tickets and the tickets quickly sold out. Sixteen-year-old Isa didn't manage to get tickets but is hoping that she will get the opportunity to see them while they are in Spain. 'We are proud of where we come from because the boys love Spain and in an interview they said that Spain was a place that will always be in their hearts,' she says. 'If I don't meet them in 2013, I won't give up hope. I will meet them one day.'

ESTHER'S STORY

Esther is 15 and from Arroyomolinos, a small town on the outskirts of Madrid. Her favourite 1D song is

'Same Mistakes'. Her best Directioner friend is called Irene; they live far away from each other so keep in contact on Facebook. They like to stay up really late watching the boys on award shows and chatting to one another.

Esther says, 'One day, Twitter was crazy about a possible One Direction visit to Spain. I thought it was a rumour but, when a radio announcer confirmed it, I got nervous and excited. I was smiling for two weeks, waiting anxiously for their arrival to my country. But I had a problem one day before they came. The TV programme *El Hormiguero* announced they would be appearing on the Halloween programme. The TV studios were too far away for me to travel on my own, so I needed someone go with me, but no one would. Irene couldn't come to Madrid and my friends wanted to go out. "It's Halloween!" they said. I was so upset and went to bed crying myself to sleep.

'My sister works in Madrid and the next day she rang me to say that Harry, Niall, Liam, Louis and Zayn were staying in the hotel where she works – the Eurostars Madrid Tower hotel. I decided that I didn't want to miss out and so, as soon as I got home from work, I got changed and jumped on the bus for the hour-long journey into the centre of Madrid.

'I met a girl on the metro called Andrea. She had a photo of One Direction as her mobile's screensaver, so

I guessed she was Directioner. I was talking with her when we arrived at the TV studios, where I saw hundreds of girls screaming and crying. I didn't understand why as the boys hadn't even arrived yet. Andrea was allowed into the building because one of her friends was taking dancing lessons there and so invited me to go with her to see behind the set where the boys would be later. I felt so privileged. Afterwards we had to make our way back outside to see the boys arrive.'

Esther and Andrea saw the boys arrive in their cars and then the boys went inside to film the programme. They had to wait outside with the other fans. After an hour, the boys appeared at an open window and waved at the girls waiting for them. Esther felt like she was dreaming – she was seeing them for real, rather than on a computer screen, for the first time.

Since that day, Esther has been to many 1D events and is currently rehearsing for a flash mob, which is happening in the summer. The fans in Spain regularly meet up and play games together and chat about 1D. At their last meeting there were more than 110 girls and boys there. She was so excited when she found out they would be performing in Spain on 24 May 2013 and rushed out to get a ticket.

She says, 'I think Spanish fans are different to the other Directioners because we are so dedicated even though we get to see them hardly ever. We still support them, because they deserve it. We have to wait all night to watch them on USA TV programmes or see their tweetcams. It is crazy to buy a CD when you do not know if its singers are real! Spanish Directioners have to translate all their interviews, songs and thank-you videos too, which can be very time consuming.

'Even without understanding them, living in the same time zone or seeing them every month, we stay being Directioners!'

ISABEL'S STORY

Isabel is 17 and from Soria in northern Spain. Her favourite song is 'One Thing' and she has a weakness for Niall. She attends the Spanish fan conventions and her first One Direction concert was in May 2013 for *Take Me Home*. She met the boys for the first time on 31 October 2012. She says, 'It was the first time they were in Spain as a group, to promote their album, so I was really excited. The previous day, it had been announced who had won the Go1Den Ticket but it wasn't me – I had been dreaming about it for weeks so I was really sad to find out that I hadn't won. All wasn't lost though: my mom gave me permission to go to the hotel they were staying at during their visit to Spain, so I thought I still might get a chance to see them.'

Isa arrived at the hotel at 9.30am with her friends, knowing that they would have a long wait ahead of them. Isa recalls, 'We passed the whole morning talking with the press, TV or anyone who passed by. I talked with Anne Igartiburu, a Spanish TV host, and I gave her a letter from my best friend to the boys. She told me she'd give it to them during the interview she was doing with them in the hotel. When she came back outside afterwards, she told me the boys had the letter. Even after waiting for five hours, I still didn't know if I would be able to see them, but knowing they had the letter made me really happy.

'The hours passed by and we were still there waiting for them, doing everything their security said we had to do. We wanted to see them even if it was behind a fence. We were so cold that we even asked one of the security men if he had a spare blanket but he just walked away laughing, thinking we were joking. Finally, at 7pm, some men started to put more fences up and told us to sit on the ground and that, if we did that, they'd come out. I've never seen a crowd sit down so quickly before.'

Finally, they began to see movement inside the hotel and Niall came outside, yelling, 'YEAH!' and just being playful. 'I've always told myself that I wouldn't be one of the fans who yells when they see the boys,' says Isa, 'but I couldn't help it, it was too amazing.

'After Niall, there was Liam and Zayn, waving in every direction, and Louis and Harry messing around. They were all smiling a lot; it turned out that they had wanted to come out to see us since the morning but hadn't been allowed. They began to salute us, and all I could think about was, "They are real, they are here, they aren't a dream, I'm dying." Then they came to the side where I was just behind the fence in the front row. A group at my right started singing the chorus of "Live While We're Young" and Louis told them to sing louder while Harry blew kisses at everyone. Niall, Zayn and Liam greeted us all.

'Then I came up with the worst idea ever. I wasn't thinking logically. I put my head between two bars of the fence (thankfully, it didn't get stuck) and, with my hand, started gesturing to the boys. Liam saw me and started laughing and copying my hand gestures. Harry blew a kiss at me and it felt unbelievable. Their security men tried to get the boys back in the hotel but the fans by me started singing "Live While We're Young" again and Niall came over and told us to sing louder, so we did. And when we finished, he yelled, "YEAH!" again before a security man took him indoors.

'As soon as they had gone, we all hugged each other,

whether we knew each other or not. We cried with excitement about what had just happened but also with a bit of sadness because it was over. As I made my way to the hotel with my friends, my face was hurting because I had been smiling so much!'

CHAPTER TWENTY-THREE

SWEDEN

When One Direction visited Sweden in February 2012, Niall tweeted, 'Sweden you legends! Mad day in stockholm! All the interviews n stuff! And directioners everywhere! #1Dinsweden'. Swedish fans loved his message and it was soon trending.

The boys have spent quite a bit of time in Sweden recording for their albums. When they were in the country recording tracks for *Take Me Home*, Niall tweeted, 'Great day soo far in the studio!! Got some crackin tunes on the way!.. its been a while since we've been in the studio..great t be back'.

Liam explained to Swedish TV channel SVT how things have changed now they have been to Sweden lots of times. 'When we went there the first time, it was fairly quiet over there, you know,' he said. 'We had a few fans and that turn up at the airport and then, when we kept going back and back, there were just more and more people coming outside the studio. By the end of it, there was, like, 500 people outside the hotel every single day, just there all night, all day.'

Zayn was really surprised they had Swedish fans to begin with because he didn't think they would know who they were. The boys have since done signings over in Sweden and Liam can remember one fan who fainted four times when she saw them. She fainted once, was taken away to recover, came back, fainted again, was taken away, came back, fainted again ... FOUR times!

DID YOU KNOW?

'One Thing' nearly didn't make it onto their *Up All Night* album. Niall told *The Ralphie Radio Show* in the US, 'We actually nearly had the album finished and "One Thing" was one of the last songs we recorded. We actually flew to Sweden just to do "One Thing" and "I Wish" 'cause we felt this was a cracking song and we needed to record it, so it was actually one of the last songs. It's like the perfect like "cousin" to "What Makes You Beautiful". It's the same kinda

---

vibe, a really punchy chorus so, you know, we just wanted to make another good song.'

SOFIA'S STORY

Sofia is 15 and from Köping in central Sweden. She was one of the boys' first fans in Sweden and has met them three times. The first time she met them was on 20 July 2011 when they were in Sweden to record their first album. Sofia only discovered them after seeing their *X Factor* performances on YouTube; they weren't famous in Sweden at that time.

'My friend Alice and I got permission from our parents to take the train up to Stockholm to try and meet the boys,' Sofia says. 'We took the early train and we went to their hotel. We waited outside for about two to three hours before Harry came outside. Seeing him seriously felt like a dream. He honestly stood 10 centimetres from me and I could see every bit of his face and it just felt unreal. He signed some autographs and took some photos. I also asked him to sign my shoe, but neither of us had a pen (I really should have brought one with me) so he couldn't do it, but it didn't matter because I would get another chance later. When he took a cab to the studio, me, Alice and all the other fans went there too. We ran there as fast as we could and, as soon as we arrived, the boys came out from the studio. They took photos and signed autographs and just had a chat with the fans. They were so wonderful! I got a high-five from all of the boys and that totally made my whole life!

'Alice and I spent the whole day outside the studio and the hotel together with 20 other fans. The boys came out to say hello every once in a while and they were all so friendly and funny! We took the train home at midnight and we were just so happy and thankful for that experience, and we still are. I just hope every fan gets to meet the boys at least once in their lives, because I got the chance to do that and I will remember that day for the rest of my life!'

The second time Sofia met the boys was at the Bring 1D to Me event. She was supposed to go with Alice that time too but, sadly, Alice got sick and couldn't come. But the event was on 2 October, which is also Sofia's birthday, so her parents gave her the trip up to Stockholm for the event as a birthday present. When Sofia and her family arrived at the location to get the wristbands that you needed to be allowed in, it was complete chaos! There were policemen everywhere and everyone was going crazy. At last, the fans managed to make a line-up and Sofia happened to come almost last. She figured out that she wouldn't get a wristband, and that fact totally broke her heart.

'Even though I was 99 per cent sure that I wouldn't get the chance to see the boys that day, I didn't give up,' Sofia recalls. 'That one per cent kept me going. It sounds clichéd but the boys have taught us to not give up and just keep going, and that was exactly what I did.'

When all the wristbands were gone and Sofia was left without one, Sofia and her mum and dad walked to Café Opera where the event would take place later that day. They created two line-ups outside the small venue: one for the fans with wristbands and one for the fans without. After a long wait, the lucky fans with wristbands got to go into the venue where they were going to meet the boys. Sofia says, ' As I stood outside Café Opera with the other fans, we asked the people who were working at this event if there was any chance at all that we could somehow get in even if we didn't have wristbands. The answer we got was something like, "There is a very, very, very small chance and, if I were you, I would go home and have a nice family dinner instead."'

Some of the fans left, but Sofia didn't give up and, after a long wait, she finally got in. 'I'm not one of those fans who normally cries when they meet their idol, but this time I did,' Sofia says, 'I told them I loved them so much and they all replied something like, "I love you too, babe," and they gave me a hug.

I am SO happy that I didn't leave after I didn't get a wristband, so a tip to all other fans – don't ever give up, even if there is a 0.00001 per cent chance that you'll meet them, don't give up!'

The third time Sofia met them was with her friend Alice again. It was on *The X Factor* Sweden and that was the first time she heard them perform live. 'When the boys announced that they were coming to Sweden to perform, I just thought, "Oh My God, I need to get tickets!" Sofia says. 'There was such a pressure while trying to get tickets because literally every teenage girl wanted one. I made my mum, dad and my brother Simon sit with a computer to try to get tickets and I was so nervous. Somehow, I was the only one in my family to succeed with the tickets. I called Alice right away and told her that we had tickets and we freaked out together on the phone! It was such an experience to be at the *X Factor* live show together with my best friend to see One Direction perform live. They were amazing, as always, and I will never forget that day!'

CHAPTER TWENTY-FOUR

UNITED KINGDOM

The UK will always be important to Harry, Liam, Louis and Zayn because Harry is from Holmes Chapel, Liam is from Wolverhampton, Louis is from Doncaster and Zayn is from Bradford. The UK is also significant to Niall because they became a band on the UK *X Factor* and he lives in London now when he's not touring with the boys. All the boys have made London their new home.

When *Up All Night* was released, it sold 138,163 copies in the UK in its first week of release, just behind Rihanna's *Talk That Talk* album, which sold 163,819 copies. Their first single, 'What Makes You Beautiful', was the most pre-ordered single Sony had ever had at the time. It was number one on iTunes within 15 minutes, knocking Maroon 5's 'Moves Like Jagger' down to second place.

> **DID YOU KNOW?**
> The front cover of *Up All Night* was taken from a photo shoot that the boys did at Camber Sands, East Sussex. It was a natural shot of them just having fun on the beach.

The first tour the boys did was The X Factor Tour with the finalists from the show. They got to sing five songs in every show. They had a great time but their Up All Night Tour was far better: they didn't have to share the stage anymore. Their first show was in Wolverhampton on 21 December 2011 and then it moved to Manchester, Bournemouth, Birmingham, Plymouth, Nottingham, Brighton, London, Glasgow, Liverpool, Newcastle, Blackpool, Sheffield, Cardiff, Dublin, and ended in Belfast on 26 January. Fans rushed out to get tickets and the tour was a sell-out, with some people paying £100 or more for tickets on eBay.

Harry told the backstage cameras, 'I think for us the highlights of the tour have been the audiences. The audiences have been just so enthusiastic and really got involved. So it's been good that they've been a part of the whole show, the whole experience.'

One of the boys' favourite UK concerts was their final night in London on 22 January 2012. Zayn tweeted, 'London!! Smashed it amazing show thank you directioners never fail to impress me with their lung capacity u guys can scream! #amazingfans!'

Niall told his followers, 'London incredible tonight! Off t chill now! Cant wait t sleep'.

In February 2012, it was announced they would be doing a UK and Ireland Arena Tour in 2013 (this was to become The World Tour). Initially, there were only 15 dates planned but, after the tickets sold out minutes after going on sale, the boys tweeted that they were adding more dates. They added an extra 20 days and they too quickly sold out.

DID YOU KNOW?

During the tour, the boys were supported by American alternative-rock band Boyce Avenue. When their UK dates finished, the Boyce Avenue boys presented them with customised Baby Taylor guitars with '1D & BA' on the back and their autographs. The guitars were an expensive gift: they would have cost Boyce Avenue a hefty £20,000 (about $31,000).

> ### DID YOU KNOW?
> When they started out, one of the boys' rituals was to line up five sweets and each of them would eat one. But, after about a month, they forgot to do it.

One of the boys' scariest moments with fans happened when they were at Heathrow airport. They confessed all to Maude Apatow from *Teen Vogue*.

Liam said, 'We were in Heathrow once, and there were about 500 girls at the airport. We went out the side door to try to get to our car but we couldn't get to it. Zayn's hoodie got ripped off. I got a good whack in the face.' Zayn added, 'There was a security booth outside and it was all glass. People were licking the windows. It felt like we were in a zombie movie.'

Once a fan asked if she could lick Liam's face, which he found really odd. Louis thinks the girl should have gone for it: 'If I was a fan and I actually had the wish to lick Liam's face, I wouldn't ask. 'Cause you know what the answer's gonna be. I would have just gone for it.'

The boys' biggest performance ever was during the Closing Ceremony of the 2012 London Olympic Games. They performed 'What Makes You Beautiful' on top of a lorry as it circled the inside of the Olympic Stadium. Zayn debuted a blonde band in his quiff, which fans instantly loved.

After their performance, Niall tweeted, 'That was unbelievable, highlight of our career, and the biggest audience we will ever play to one billion people! #ThankYouLondon2012'.

> **DID YOU KNOW?**
>
> The boys had all-access passes at the Olympics, and they used them to sneak away from their security team. They went to the top of the Orbit tower and they went to the Aquatics Centre even though it was closed to the public at the time. They also watched a water polo match – and teased their security team by sending them photos.

The boys might have filmed their first two videos in America but they filmed their third in London. (One Direction's third single in the UK and Ireland was 'One Thing'. It was their second release in other countries.) Harry, Niall, Liam, Louis and Zayn filmed the video on 28 November 2011. Fans were invited to take part for the scenes in Trafalgar Square and the boys had a blast just messing around.

Louis told Real Radio the concept: 'Basically, there

wasn't much of a script for the video … it was more like, we're going to go to these different locations, be yourself, do what you want to do and, for me, it's our, probably, most real and more like us video that we've had so far – it worked really well.'

Harry tweeted the next day, 'Big thanks to everyone who got involved in our video yesterday!! It was fun, and hopefully you'll like it. Video 3…done!'

DID YOU KNOW?

Harry's mum says Harry's bedroom in London isn't the neatest. She told the *People*, 'In Harry's bedroom there are clothes everywhere, posters from clothes shops, trendy things from catalogues. He has a brown and cream colour scheme but the clothes are everywhere. He's pretty messy, it is his worst habit.'

Harry and Zayn have both bought houses near each other in an exclusive part of London. Harry's house has a double car lift, four bedrooms, three reception rooms and three bathrooms. It is rumoured to have cost him £3 million!

The boys filmed the video for 'Live While We're Young', their first release from their second album, in the Kent countryside over two days. Harry tweeted, 'Great day shooting for the music video for "Live While We're Young" bit nippy...'

The video was directed by Vaughan Arnell and it had a happy, celebratory feel to it. The boys wake up in a huge tent at the start of the video and then have fun with their friends around a camp. Louis drives them around in a Jeep, they have water fights, play in a pool, play football, swing off a rope swing ... basically, have lots of fun! Niall is there, strumming his guitar, and even appears without a top on – Harry, Liam, Louis and Zayn just keep their wet shirts on.

After filming finished, Niall tweeted, 'Guys! We have literally just finished shooting the video for "live while we're young" ur gona love it! It was soo fun to shoot!'

Harry also tweeted his followers, 'Day two finished, and that's the video for 'Live While We're Young' done. Amazing crew, amazing people involved. Thanks again.'

The video was supposed to be shown on 24 September 2012 for the first time but, a few weeks earlier, photos from the video were leaked and then, on 20 September, a rough version of the video was posted online. This upset the boys as they didn't want fans to see something that wasn't perfect. They decided to release the official version that day instead and said in a statement, 'We wanted our fans to see the video and hear the single in the proper way so we've moved the première to tonight. We're really excited about LWWY, we've worked really hard on it and we can't wait for everyone to see and hear it later today!'

DID YOU KNOW?

'Live While We're Young' was written by Savan Kotecha, Rami Yacoub and Carl Falk, who had written/produced 'What Makes You Beautiful'.

'Live While We're Young' became the fastest selling pre-order single ever. It was number one in 40 countries worldwide! The boys' PR company released a statement on their website stating, '"Live While We're Young" is pop perfection – an immediate, energy packed song mixing rock undertones with smooth harmonies, about living for the moment.'

Niall tweeted, 'Thanks for the love for LWWY, we

have worked hard on this album, hope u enjoy the rest of it'.

SHANNICE'S STORY

Shannice is 15 and from London. She first met the boys when they appeared on the *Alan Carr: Chatty Man show*. It was their first TV interview after *The X Factor*. She has met them many times, as she goes to the TV studios in London whenever she knows they will be appearing on a chat or game show.

She explains what it was like the first time she met them: 'I thought they weren't going to come out because it got so dark and late, but they did. Their security team kept telling them they had to go but they just ignored them. Liam said to me, "I have the same jumper as you, it's cool," which he probably did, as it was a men's jumper from a JJB Sports store!

'All the times I've been to the studios since, they have come out, signed things, taken pictures and generally tried their best to please all the fans, which is so nice of them. One time Louis took a photo of me and Liam, and another time Zayn took a photo of us together. The photo Zayn took is a bit blurry but I don't mind.'

If you want to follow Shannice on Twitter, her Twitter name is @onedirection_ZM.

ELLIE'S STORY

Ellie is 15 and from Liverpool. She met One Direction on 22 October 2012 in Doncaster, where Louis took part in a charity football match. She says, 'I went with my friends Rosa, Neave and Jocelyn. It took nearly five hours to get there but it was so worth it the second we saw Harry pull into the car park and get out of his car. He waved for a while before going inside. Soon after, Niall and Liam pulled in and did the same. Eventually, Louis came and he kindly came round and took pictures with loads of fans at the barriers, including us. He was so sweet and really polite, despite the fact people were screaming in his face.

'The match was so much fun to watch, and we even got to speak to Harry, Liam and Niall really hurriedly before it started. We had a really good time, and the screaming every time Louis got the ball was *insane*. At the end of the match there was a penalty shootout, and everyone was so gutted when Louis missed, but they let him take another shot and he scored. I have never heard screaming like that, not even in a concert. The fact that this was all organised for charity made it even better, and it was such a good idea. It was such a great night, worth all the travelling!'

DANIELLE'S STORY

Danielle is a fan from Glasgow and she also went to Louis' football match, as well as seeing the boys perform in Glasgow. She doesn't mind having to travel to see Harry, Niall, Liam, Louis and Zayn. She thinks that the atmosphere at a 1D concert is amazing and they sound even better live.

MEGAN'S STORY

Megan is 16 and from Brighton. She has met the boys twice: once at a signing for their book *Dare to Dream* and then at their Brighton tour date on the 8 January 2012. At the Brighton concert, she got to go backstage because her friend Georgia had been Harry's Radio 1 Star Caller a few months earlier. Georgia had entered a competition to have Harry ring her and he had done, while she was in a science class at school. While he was on the phone, she had the opportunity to ask him one question, and she asked if she and Megan could meet them on the tour. Megan takes up the story:

'He said yes and asked what date we were going to and said we will keep in contact and sort something out. And, of course, we went absolutely crazy with joy because we already had third row tickets, and to get to meet them was a dream come true again!'

On the day of the concert, Megan and Georgia had to pick up special wristbands from the reception at 7pm. When they arrived, the receptionist called someone to take them up to the room where they would be meeting Harry, Niall, Liam, Louis and Zayn. 'We entered the room to be greeted by Liam sitting with another fan and her mum and with his girlfriend Danielle,' Megan recalls. 'He greeted me by saying, "Hey, babe," and I said hello and gave him a cookie that said "Love from Georgia and Megan', and he said, "Aw, thanks, babe, I'll make sure the other boys see it."

Megan and Georgia had a photo taken with him and then they got to meet Harry, Niall and Louis. Megan gave both Niall and Louis a kiss on their cheeks but, when she pulled away from Louis, her hair got caught in his stubble, which was funny. She told him, 'Maybe you should go have a shave,' which made him laugh. Sadly, Zayn didn't come into the room but the girls got to meet the boys' drummer Josh and had a photo taken with him too. He was smaller than Megan because she was wearing heels, so he had to stand on his tiptoes and she had to bend down a bit to make it look like they were the same size

KATIE'S STORY

Katie is 14 and from Essex. She has met the boys twice in London but admits she's never been as nervous as she was the first time she met them. 'I was shaking uncontrollably,' she says. 'I couldn't believe that they were really standing right in front of me. I couldn't say anything, I was in complete shock, still shaking as each of the boys tried to make conversation, saying hello and asking me how I was. All I could say was, "Hello, I'm really good, thanks." Once it was over, I was so annoyed with myself. I wish that I had spoken more.'

Katie made sure that when she met them for the second time at Lakeside Shopping Centre she was prepared and didn't waste the opportunity. She brought a fan book she had made and gave it to Zayn, who was really chuffed.

AMY'S STORY

Amy is 15 and from Halifax. She met the boys on 16 August 2011 in Leeds while they were promoting 'What Makes You Beautiful' at a local radio station. Her advice to fans going to meet the boys is to take a camera so you can take as many photos as possible. 'When Niall started waving at me from their car, I think my heart stopped!' she confesses. 'My hands were shaking like crazy, and I was capturing as many memories as I could as they all climbed out and started walking in my direction.'

She was so excited when Harry agreed to have a photo taken with her. 'He put his arm round my back, just touching my waist, while my arm was clasping his waist,' she says. 'My mum was taking the photo, so I went to look at it and, to my disbelief, she hadn't taken the photo!'

Thankfully, Harry didn't mind doing it again, otherwise Amy's mum would have been in big trouble.

JENNA'S STORY

Jenna is 17 and from South Shields. She has met the boys twice and Niall even sent her a Christmas card! Jenna explains how she came to get a card: 'Well, I spoke to his dad's girlfriend, Aofie; we had been in touch lots and lots through Skype and Facebook. My friend's mam knew her too and thought, as a Christmas present, getting something signed for us would be really nice. So they got in touch and sent over Christmas cards for me and my friend. Luckily, the day they arrived at Niall's home, he had a couple of days off. Well, Aofie wanted them to be personal and took into consideration things we spoke about.

Well, we always joked on about Niall having a poo face, so she told Niall that and that's why he wrote "you smell off poo poo" inside the card, and he wrote "gocky" in my friend's because he always used to say it.

'As for meeting them, I met them in Newcastle on The X Factor Tour and I met them in Leeds during their radio tour. When I met them in Leeds, Niall gave me a doughnut and we got a photo together. He signed a poster I had made for him and we chatted with Zayn about giraffes because I have an obsession with them and Niall said he only liked giraffes because I did.'

REBECCA'S STORY

Rebecca is 16 and from Cardiff. She met the boys when they were doing the X Factor Tour at the Motorpoint Arena. She decided to get there early and wait outside in case she could see them. She had to wait hours and hours but they did eventually come out to speak to her and the other fans that were there.

'When they came out, I couldn't believe my eyes,' she says. 'They were playing football in the arena. Their rules were that they weren't allowed outside unless they were playing football. They weren't allowed to meet the fans. One Direction, being One

Direction, didn't stick to that rule though. They kept coming to the fans and signing autographs, taking pictures and being dragged away. I remember just watching Liam walk over to me. He was looking directly into my eyes. Everybody was screaming but I was too mesmerised by *that* actually being Liam Payne to scream. And with that, he came straight to me and began to sign my autograph, smiling that huge smile he always does. Then, before he moved on, I managed to burst out with, "I love you, Liam." And he looked back to me, smiled and said, "I love you too."

'From then on, the crowds grew, yet the boys continued to try their best to meet us. Louis came over and signed an autograph for me, and I managed to stroke his hand (weird, I know!). Harry also began to mimic me, smiling, blowing kisses, waving, just doing what I was basically doing. They were so lovely. I gave them footballs and they were SO grateful. They started playing about with them and I couldn't remove the smile from my face.'

HANNAH'S STORY

Hannah is 17 and from Norfolk. She first met the boys outside the Channel 4 TV studios in London with her friends Adrianne and Lauren. There were so many fans waiting there for them that, when they caught a glimpse of the boys through a fence, it all went a bit crazy. Hannah and Lauren had brought some presents for the boys but the only way to get them to them was by throwing them. Hannah explains, 'I had made an I LOVE NANDO'S T-shirt for Niall the day before meeting them and was determined to get it to him. So Lauren threw the T-shirt through the fence and it hit Niall on the head, but he caught it and blew a kiss to her. I was so excited Niall had his T-shirt, but I was still determined to get the rest of the presents through, so I threw the other presents over the fence for them to pick up.'

Once the boys had gone inside, Hannah and Lauren decided to go for a wander around London for a couple of hours to calm down and have an ice cream. They figured the boys would be a while filming – they were right. When they got back, they waited right by the fence, and made some new friends. 'While we were waiting, everyone was singing and chanting,' Hannah remembers. 'It really was amazing meeting and being around all these girls who had so much in common with you.

'After about four hours the boys came out and the screams were really loud. I was pushed up against the fence by loads of girls but I was prepared: I had my phone case, what I wanted Niall to sign, my notepad and a pen. Liam came up to us first and I got his autograph, and my friend gave him one of my sharpies, which he thanked her for. Then Niall came up to us. I was so excited. I gave him my phone to sign and he signed the case and then I asked him if he got the Nando's T-shirt and he said, "Yes, thank you, I'm going to wear it tomorrow!" At that moment I didn't care if he was lying – he still got it! I got autographs from Zayn, Louis, Liam and Niall that day; Harry didn't really come up to us as he stayed up the other end, but I was so happy.'

When the boys had gone back inside, Hannah and Lauren made their way back to the train station, but it was so late that they missed the last train home. Thankfully, Hannah's dad came to pick them up – otherwise they would've been stranded.

When Hannah woke up the next day, it felt like it had been all a dream. She went on Twitter because Niall was doing an #AskNiall so fans could ask him anything they wanted: 'He mentioned my T-shirt on an answer to someone. It said, "Yes I love Nando's one of the beautiful girls from yesterday gave me an I Love Nando's T-shirt!" He called me beautiful, so my life was made!'

If you want to follow Hannah on Twitter, her Twitter name is @hannaa_26.

ELEANOR'S STORY

When 16-year-old Eleanor from Sheffield read a tweet from Liam saying, 'I love these squidgy things there amazing' with a photo of him holding a bright yellow rubber face ball with blue hair, she couldn't help but smile. She was one of 118 fans who tweeted him back, telling him that, if he ever came to her hometown, she would give him a squidgy ball, not thinking she would receive a response. But she did. He tweeted back, 'Love that, thank you babe J'. Eleanor rushed out, bought him an orange one with green hair, and couldn't wait to give it to him in person one day.

Why not follow Eleanor on Twitter? Her account is @Nouis_Toran. She has around 7,000 followers on Twitter, including Liam himself!

EMILY'S STORY

Emily is 16 years old and from London. If you own the *Take Me Home* Limited Edition Yearbook, flick over to the fans page to see a photo of Emily with Niall: she is wearing a pink top and Niall has his arm around her. The photo was taken on 15 September 2011 at their *Dare to Dream* book signing in a shopping centre in Thurrock in Essex. Emily explains what happened:

'I was just about to meet the boys, but their management told the boys to take a five-minute break, as they had been sitting for quite a while signing books. As they were having their break, they were messing around and interacting with the screaming fans. The boys were also filming footage for their *A Year in the Making* documentary for ITV2 and Louis stood on his chair and took a camera from the crew. He started to film the fans on all three levels of the shopping centre, the queues on the floor, and then he leaned down and put the camera on me – I was so happy! I was standing behind Niall so he basically filmed me and Niall!

'Later on, Liam and Niall were sitting and standing on the table. When Niall climbed off the table, he dropped the sharpie he was signing books with; he was looking around on the floor for his pen and, because I was in the first row, I shouted out, "Niall, your pen!" and pointed to where the pen was lying. He walked over, picked it up, and then came over to me and kneeled on the stage and over the barrier to thank me. He gave me a hug and a kiss on my cheek. I was so shocked and I was in hysterics. Not only did I get a hug and kiss from him, I also got my picture taken. I was the only person Niall took a picture with during the break! I couldn't believe it when the photo appeared in the Yearbook.'

MAISIE'S STORY

Maisie is 15 and from London. Maisie has met the boys lots of times outside their recording studio in London. Every time she meets them she gets butterflies in her tummy. 'They are such genuine, lovely boys who really care a lot about their fans and always take the time to meet them,' she says. 'I hope everyone gets a chance to meet them because, if you love them as much as I do, it really will be the best and most memorable experience of your life!

'Once when I was at the studio, Louis came out with a towel on his head hoping we wouldn't recognise him, but his bright red chinos and stripy top kind of gave him away. Another time, Niall kept peeping his head out of the car door and jumping in and out of it, playing around. They're always up for a good laugh and enjoy messing around with the fans.'

CIARA'S STORY

When 16-year-old Ciara met One Direction with her friends, she gave them loads of toys and stuff just for fun, like pink feather boas, power rangers, swords and kid's balls. They all played around with them and Ciara found it so funny. They gave Harry some pink hair rollers as a joke and he put them in his hair!

Ciara says, 'It makes me so happy knowing I've met them and I am very grateful.

After many more failed attempts to meet them again in 2012, in October I attended Louis' charity football match and met him outside before the game and he signed my *Up All Night* album.

'They're such nice boys, I just wish I had the opportunity to meet them more often. A lot of the times you go to see them outside hotels and concerts they just get in their tour bus and drive away because they're in a rush or there are too many people.'

CHARLOTTE'S STORY

Charlotte is 16 and lives in Essex. She never expected to meet the boys on her way to an appointment at the Great Ormond Street Hospital with her mother. She thought they were in America, but she was wrong.

Charlotte and her mother were early, so decided to go to Milkshake City – the place where One Direction like to go for their milkshakes when they are in London. Milkshake City has lots of photos of Harry, Liam, Louis, Niall and Zayn on its wall, as well as photos of JLS, famous footballers and Kimberley Walsh from Girls Aloud. They even sell a One Direction milkshake, which contains Dime bar, Twix, chocolate digestives, Jammie Dodgers, a secret ingredient, and has Millions Bubblegum on the top. (There is one flavour for each member of the band.)

On their way to Milkshake City, Charlotte recognised the gates to Princess Park Manor where One Direction were living at the time. Harry and Louis were living in one apartment and the other three boys were living in another, paid for by their record label. She decided to see if she could get a closer look, and her mother came along too. The building's security guard chatted to them and, after they'd had a quick look around, he asked if Charlotte would like to leave a message for the boys and told her to go to reception. Before she could, he admitted that Harry might still be in the building because he could see his car, parked a way to the left. Charlotte and her mother decided to have a look at it but, as they got closer, they realised that Harry was right there, next to his car. Charlotte couldn't believe it! Harry turned and smiled at them. He then said, 'Hello, ladies,' which Charlotte describes as 'the moment my heart melted. I had no idea what to do. I couldn't think to save my life.' All she could reply was, 'Hiya, Harry.' Here's the conversation that followed:

Mum: 'Why, hello, Harry, aren't you polite?'

Harry: 'Hello, what's your name (to Charlotte)? Ahh thanks (to Charlotte's mother).'

Charlotte: 'Um, I'm Charlotte.'

Harry: 'What a lovely name Charlotte is! I like that name. One of Louis' sisters is called Charlotte and it's a very pretty name. Sooo, what you doing here?'

Mum: 'Well, Charlotte has a hospital appointment at Great Ormond Street and we were on our way to Milkshake City, then we spoke to security and they said come down if you want.'

Harry: 'Aww, what do you have to go to the hospital for, Charlotte? And, yes, Milkshake City is the best! I love it there!'

Charlotte: 'Well, umm, I have bad migraines and I go there!'

Harry: 'Aww, you poor thing! Come here (he stepped forward and gave Charlotte a hug and a kiss on the cheek!). Have you got anything you want signing?'

Luckily, Charlotte had a 1D CD in her bag, so Harry signed that and then he asked if she wanted a photo, so her mother took one with her phone. The boy's hair stylist, Lou Teasdale, came outside and Harry told them he would be back in a minute; he just needed to take his washing inside.

While he was gone, Charlotte and her mother had a nice chat to Lou about the tour and then Harry snuck up on Charlotte, shouted, 'Boo!' and then started laughing. He apologised, saying, 'Sorry for that. I'm just so excited for America!' Charlotte started giggling and replied, 'It's OK! And you must be! I would be too!'

Charlotte's mother then said, 'OK, we had better be off, I think we are going to Milkshake City next... Umm, do you know where it is 'cause I don't have a clue?'

Harry smiled, said he loved Milkshake City and then gave them some directions so they would be able to find it. As they turned to go, Charlotte went to say goodbye but Harry spoke first, saying, 'Oh, yes, forgot to say, thanks so much for helping us get The Brit. It's all down to people like you! And did you hear us say about the tour next year?'

Charlotte couldn't believe Harry was thanking her for being a fan, and told him, 'Aww, that's OK, you and the boys deserve it. And, yes, I'm on O2, so I get priority, so will hopefully get some tomorrow.'

'Ahh, cool! I wish I could buy some, but I'm at work! I think it would be a great show to see!' Harry joked.

Her mother teased, 'Ah, well, I'm sure they may let you have a seat on the stage for free.'

Harry laughed and said, 'Ah, yes, we can't wait already and it's 366 days to go!'

As they walked away, Charlotte's parting remark to Harry was, 'It has been a dream meeting you!' and he wouldn't let her go without another hug. 'Bye, Charlotte and Charlotte's mum,' he shouted as they walked back up the drive to the main road.

Charlotte thought that was the only chance she would ever get to see Harry, but she was wrong: she got to see him again a few minutes later, as Harry, Liam and Louis went to Milkshake City for a milkshake while she was there! When Harry saw her, he pointed and said, 'Hey! Are you following me!? Haha, only joking, babe! Then Louis turned and said, 'Harry, is there something you're not telling me?'

Harry explained how they had met before and Liam signed Charlotte's CD. They were having a chat and posing for a photo, but then Liam's phone went off and it was his girlfriend, Danielle Peazer, so he moved into the corner to speak to her in private. Harry tried to get Louis to sign the CD, which he did and then his phone went off before he could have a photo. The boys had to leave but Charlotte didn't mind too much though, because Harry gave her another hug and kiss and wished her good luck at the hospital.

Today, when Charlotte thinks back to that day, she says, 'I still can't believe it happened, it was amazing. Harry smelled of sugar and aftershave! Liam smelled of popcorn and aftershave and Louis smelled of perfume and aftershave!' If you would like to follow Charlotte on Twitter, her account is @CharW1D.

EMILY'S STORY

Emily is 14 and from Liverpool. She met One Direction on Saturday, 17 September 2011. She wouldn't have been able to meet them if it hadn't been for her dad. He knew how much she wanted to see them, so volunteered to camp out for Emily and her friend Jess on the Wednesday night to get a wristband for their *Dare to Dream* book signing in Liverpool. He got there at midnight, even though the WH Smith's store wasn't open until 7am the next day. He was 30th in the queue. He had brought with him a camping chair, a few blankets and a flask of hot chocolate, but he spilled it over the chair. Emily's dad didn't get much sleep that night.

Emily woke up early the next morning, waiting for her dad to call, but he didn't. Emily really thought he must have missed out because she'd been expecting a call not long after 7am and nearly an hour had passed. She couldn't wait by the phone because she had to leave for school but, when she got outside, her dad pulled up in his car with two *Dare to Dream* books and two wristbands – he had done it! She was going to be meeting the boys two days later!

When she caught up with Jess in the playground, Emily decided to pull a prank on her and pretended that her dad hadn't got the wristbands. Emily pretended to cry and Jess fell for it, giving her a hug. Emily quickly came clean and the two of them started talking about what they were going to wear (once they had stopped screaming). Emily choose her 'I LOVE 1D' top, black leggings and red Converse, and Jess choose an 1D top with beige leggings and red Converse. It turned out that their other friend, Paige, and Emily's cousin, Alicia, had wristbands too.

The night before the signing, Jess came over to Emily's house as she was going to be sleeping there so they could go the signing together. They didn't get much sleep though; they were too excited. They rang their friend Charlie on Emily's mobile, even though it was the middle of the night, and kept looking at the clock to see how long they had left to meet Harry, Louis, Liam, Zayn and Niall. They finally went to sleep at 3am and got up at 7am to start getting ready for the book signing at 10am.

Emily's dad and mum drove them to the centre of Liverpool. It was packed because it was a Saturday but the girls needed to get a birthday card to give to Niall because it had been his 18th birthday on 13 September. After they'd got the card, they quickly wrote in it before they arrived at the secret location – The Russell Building. The girls had to wait for two hours in the pouring rain until they were allowed in. While they were waiting, Liam and Louis hung their heads out of the window and waved to the waiting fans. Loads of people screamed, including Emily and Jess; they were going to meet them after dreaming about it for so long. The girls spotted Harry's dad Des, and Emily's mum even chatted to him, telling him that Emily was smitten with Harry, and he admitted that he was the proudest dad in the world.

As they got into the lift with Emily's mum to go up to the signing, Emily and Jess clasped their hands together and kept a tight hold on their *Dare To Dream* books. It was so surreal to them, knowing that in only a matter of minutes they were going to be standing in front of One Direction. As they got out of the lift, they could see their friend Paige up ahead, standing in front of her favourite member, Zayn. She started crying, but then Louis went under the table and jumped back up with a mask on to cheer her up! All the fans couldn't help but start to laugh.

DID YOU KNOW?

Harry's mum, sister, cousin Ella, Zayn's sisters and Zayn's mum were there that day too. Superfan Olivia shared a lift with them and says, 'When we were in the lift, my friend didn't realise who they were, so I texted her subtly and then we started laughing. I said, "Hi," to Anne because I

---

used to talk to her on Twitter, but I didn't speak to the others as we were only in the lift for about three minutes.'

When it was finally their turn, Emily and Jess were nervously laughing, and Zayn was too. The security guard took their books and put them on the table. The seating order was Zayn, Louis, Liam, Niall, and then Emily's favourite, Harry, last. She passed her camera to her mum to make sure she captured it all. When they got to Louis, Emily passed him a note from her friend Poppy and then they spent a while chatting to Liam. He asked them if they were OK and stroked Emily's hand – she nearly died – she hadn't been expected him to do that and it made her blush. Jess gave Niall his card and he said thank you. He was surrounded by balloons the fans had given him and he was wearing a green flower necklace, a white skull top, blue baggy jeans and blue Supras. The girls thought the boys looked even more gorgeous in real life: Zayn was wearing a white top, a burgundy American Apparel jacket, chinos and burgundy Doc Martens; Louis was wearing a blue top, grey jeans and grey Toms; Liam was wearing a blue checked shirt, chinos and white Converse; and Harry was wearing a brown jumper, jeans and Converse.

When it came to Harry, Emily froze. 'The person who I love with all my heart was sitting there. His eyes looked at me,' she explained. '"I love you," blurted out of my mouth; he said, "I love you too," back. I couldn't believe it. I know he says that to every girl who tells him that they love him, but for that moment I was in complete awe. Paul (their security manager) then said we had to go, and we walked away, still in complete shock. We got outside the building and our mouths where still hanging open, buckets full of tears running down our cheeks. We stopped to watch our videos and the photo my mum had taken of Harry. We were still crying and this old man came up to me and Jess and asked if we were OK. We walked to the car, with our prized possessions in our hands. We couldn't believe it. It only lasted one minute, but it was the best one minute of our lives. It was the best day ever, we were so lucky.'

If you would like to follow Emily on Twitter, her Twitter account is @harrywhora.

DID YOU KNOW?

Before the signing, the boys popped into Alder Hey Children's Hospital in Liverpool to visit sick children. They wanted to help put a smile on their faces and they certainly did that. The children were thrilled to see their heroes.

ABI'S STORY

Abi is 16 and from Rochdale. She met the boys on Saturday, 17 September 2011 too. After Emily had seen them in Liverpool, they jumped in their van and headed to the Trafford Centre in Manchester for another signing. The boys are always really busy travelling to many different places so that they can see as many fans as possible.

When Abi met Louis, she gave him a picture her five-year-old sister Lily had drawn of him. She had used green crayon and Louis had three legs, but he didn't seem to mind, and he gave Abi a huge smile. The boys love receiving pictures from their fans and put some of them up in their apartments. They keep them with the fan books they receive; the boys love looking at them and appreciate the effort fans have gone to.

Abi wanted to give her sister a big surprise, so asked Louis if he could say hi to her while she recorded it on her mobile. He nodded and said, 'Hi, Lily!' and then he and Liam burst out into a chorus of 'Lily, Lily, Lily, Lily' while Niall laughed. The girl behind Abi in the line started pushing her but she held her ground and went to speak to Harry. He remembered her from when they'd met before at another event. He said, 'Hi Abi'. Abi was so touched that he'd remembered her, because he meets so many fans every day. For her it made all those times she had spent waiting in the cold for hours to see them worth it.

You can follow Abi on Twitter if you like. Her account is @abiwhitefoot.

MAGDA'S STORY

Magda is 16 and from Hayes, London. She has more than 25 different photos of herself with the boys from the various times she has met them at Heathrow Airport and in other places. In one photo, she is giving Louis a piggyback!

She says, 'It's not always easy meeting the One Direction boys. I wouldn't call it "luck" at all. I call it effort. Every single time I met them I have put effort into finding out where they are and all the relevant information. Luck would be if I randomly met them and didn't put the effort in, although I'm lucky I live near the airport because that's where I have met them most frequently. The boys are really lovely when you meet them, although paparazzi sometimes ruin it for me, my friends and other fans, as security takes them straight to the cars. It's for their own safety though. Seeing how popular the boys have become and how many more fans turn up at places makes me feel proud. I appreciate every single moment spent with them because I've got really nice memories with them. The best thing about meeting the boys is the friends you make along the way and I have made many.'

If you want to follow Magda on Twitter, her account is @1DCrew.

LAURA'S STORY

Laura is 17 and from Doncaster. She met the boys on 17 August 2011 at the Trax FM radio studio in Doncaster with her cousin Lucy and friends. They arrived there at 9am; it was a hot day so Laura got quite burned as they were waiting.

> **TOP TIP**
> Always take plenty of drinks and food with you when waiting to see the boys outside a studio. And look at the weather forecast so you can take sun cream, waterproofs or extra layers if you need them. It's a good idea to take a foldable chair too, if you can.

At approximately 3pm, Louis' mum Johannah arrived with his sisters Lottie, Felicite, Daisy and Phoebe. They didn't rush inside but came to talk to Laura and the other fans waiting. They said that Louis was on his way. A while later, a journalist came and wanted to speak to any fans that were from Doncaster and Laura was chosen.

While they were waiting for the boys, one of the fans started to feel unwell. Laura explains what happened: 'A girl stood a bit to the left of me was found by one of the police security people sat on the ground feeling faint, so an ambulance was called. Turns out she hadn't eaten all day. Louis' mum came over and asked why there was an ambulance. The policeman told her and she was, like, "Well, hasn't anyone got a Mars bar?" I know it wasn't a laughing matter, but the way she said it was funny.

'At about five past four a people carrier turned up, and by now there must have been at least 100 girls and everyone was screaming, thinking it was them. Then a woman got out and some bodyguards. It was so funny. People still thought they might be in the back (because it had blacked-out windows), so I got crushed against the barrier.

'Then I was just like looking around in confusion, and I saw the same type of people carrier driving down a different road near us. The boys went the wrong way. Haha! Two minutes later, the people carrier eventually found us, coming through the gate. Niall was sat in the front passenger seat and was the first one out.'

Laura was speechless when Harry, Liam, Louis, Zayn and Niall started walking towards her and she gripped tightly onto the fan book she had made. Liam noticed it in her hand and asked, 'You want me to take that?' He winked as he took it and their hands touched for a moment. One Direction then went inside for their radio interview, returning to meet fans afterwards.

When they did, Laura asked Zayn to sign her iPod, which he did, and then they had a photo together. Niall came over. He was hyper so gave Laura a superfast hug and signed her iPod. She also got a hug and picture from Liam, and he signed her iPod. When Louis came over, Laura managed to make him laugh. She explains what happened: 'He signed my iPod, then I got a photo with him. I have a rubbish phone, and couldn't really see the screen because of the sun, but I thought that I hadn't got him in the photo. So I asked for another one. And he was, like, "You don't ask for much, do you?" and I was, like, "Duh, I'm from Doncaster, this doesn't happen often," and he started laughing and he was, like, "Just kidding, of course you can have another."

'Turns out, both pictures were OK; the first one just cut out a bit of my head, haha.

'Then Harry came over. I'd like to say that I kept my calm and played it cool. But I'd be lying. My iPod had run out of room, so I asked him to sign my hoodie. He said, "Yeah, sure." But his pen stopped working, so he was stood in front of me for a while digging in his pockets for another pen, pulling faces at me ('cause, you know, tight trousers). I got a pic of him pulling a face: http://twitpic.com/67llc2.

'Once he'd found the pen and signed my hoodie, he leaned over me to sign a few things behind me. Harry Styles was touching me. And then everyone started really pushing. The security guard pulled him away and had a word with him. He then went to the people next to me. I asked for a picture but he'd already moved on and the security guards were, like, "No turning back." But he turned back to me and said sorry while nodding his head towards the security guards.

'It was a great day, one I won't forget. Before them, I'd never really met a celebrity, so it was amazing to meet my favourite five singers. It was also nice sharing the experience with my cousin and friends, as we'll always have that experience to remember together.'

If you want to follow Laura on Twitter, her account is @1Direction_Lver.